CONFUSION and HOPE

Clergy, Laity, and the Church in Transition

edited by GLENN RICHARD BUCHER
and PATRICIA RUTH HILL

FORTRESS PRESS   Philadelphia

Biblical quotations from the Revised Standard Version of the Bible, copyrighted 1946 and 1952 by the Division of Christian Education of the National Council of the Churches of Christ in the United States of America, are used by permission. Biblical quotations from *The New English Bible*, copyright © 1961 and 1970 by the Delegates of the Oxford University Press and the Syndics of the Cambridge University Press, are reprinted by permission. Biblical quotations from *The Jerusalem Bible*, copyright © 1966 by Darton, Longman & Todd, Ltd. and Doubleday and Company, Inc., are used by permission.

The chapter entitled "Religion, Inc." copyright © 1974 by Jeffrey K. Hadden, is used by permission. A modified version of the chapter entitled "The Cultural Captivity of the American Churches" by C. C. Goen appeared as a guest editorial in *Foundations: A Baptist Journal of History and Theology* 12 (July–September 1969), pp. 197–207. A modified version of the chapter entitled "The Believers' Church and Catholicity in the World Today" appeared in *Chicago Theological Seminary Register* (September 1970), pp. 1–9.

Library of Congress Catalog Card Number 74–76923

ISBN 0-8006-1303-1

4261 A 74   Printed in U.S.A.   1-1303

He has sent me to announce good news to the poor, to proclaim release for prisoners and recovery of sight for the blind,
to let the broken victims go free, to proclaim the year of
the Lord's favour.

Luke 4:18–19

This book is dedicated to the
hope that those clergy and
laity who are struggling to
be the church will find a way
to "proclaim the year of the
Lord's favour" in our time.

Contents

Preface   ix

PART ONE   THE CONFUSION

Introduction   3

1   Religion, Inc.   7
        Jeffrey K. Hadden

2   A Contemporary Portrait of Clergymen   17
        Edgar W. Mills and Garry W. Hesser

3   Christian Ministry in Earthen Vessels   32
        Sidney D. Skirvin

4   The Cultural Captivity of the American Churches   48
        C. C. Goen

PART TWO   THE HOPE

Introduction   73

5   Christianity: A Religion or a Way of Life?   77
        William M. Cosgrove

6   The Word: Experienced, Incarnate, Enabled   88
        A. James Armstrong

vii

7 Parish as Christian Community 100

     John E. Schramm

8 The Believers' Church and Catholicity
   in the World Today 113

     Rosemary R. Ruether

Contributors 127

Preface

This book, *Confusion and Hope: Clergy, Laity, and the Church in Transition*, is a response to three contemporary crises in American Christianity: those involving the clergy, the laity, and the parish. Stripped of their historical authority by the prevalent anti-authoritarian cynicism which characterizes much of American society today, clergy are experiencing a crisis of identity, role, and function. Simultaneously, laity within the churches increasingly are perplexed about what it means to be a Christian in an ever-more-normless culture. And as the more traditional functions of the parish are fulfilled by secular institutions and associations, the parish has been tossed into a quandary over its purpose. Indeed, confusion is a mild term for the present situation in the church. The times are pregnant with the need to address these crises.

The material included here presupposes, in addition to the fact of crisis, that these dilemmas are symbols of both confusion and hope. This predicament of the church is not particularly new; in fact St. Paul's New Testament letters, addressing problems in the early church, anticipate it. What is new, necessarily so, is the specific profile of the confusion, and the apparent despair. Part One of the book, with an accompanying introduction, is intended to address this situation, whereas Part Two, with its introduction, is an effort to renew hope in the church's ministries. If current interest in "theologies of Christian hope" is to mean anything in real life, then it must be made manifest in the lives of clergy, laity, and parishes!

The chapters which follow are, unlike much contemporary religious literature, designed for clergy and laity alike. It is time that those involved in Christian ministry, be they "professionals" or those who profess daily, begin to share their perceptions, concerns, and hopes about themselves, each other, parish life, and Christian ministry. In other words, the material, although it does assume that there is a peculiar reality to what it means to be a clergyperson or layperson, speaks to both in a mutually inclusive manner. Perhaps the book will even provide the basis upon which clergy and laity sit down together and speak what is actually on their minds. Such an encounter cannot occur without hope—hope that beyond the current confusions, disappointments, and frustrations with one another and the church, God will continue to recreate his servants for new tasks in an ever-changing world within which he continues to act in redemptive love.

The book is a direct result of the Clergy Academy of Religion, an eight-week continuing education program for Protestant and Roman Catholic clergy, held at The College of Wooster in Wooster, Ohio. Sponsored by the Department of Religion and a Clergy Academy Board, the Seventh Annual Academy attracted seventy-five clergy from northeast Ohio who came together to consider the theme, "The Struggle for Humanness: Challenges and Possibilities for New Models of Servanthood."

Major presentations and small group discussions constituted the program's format. In the following manner and with the assistance of these guests, the theme was defined and discussed: "Leaves from the Notebook of a Parish Clergyman" with Father John H. Archibald, Holy Family Roman Catholic Church, Stow, Ohio; "Why Pastors Leave the Parish: Confessions of Ex-Clergy" with Dean Sidney D. Skirvin, Union Seminary, New York; "Christianity as Faith and Clergy as Servants: A Sociological View" with Professor Jeffrey K. Hadden, Department of Anthropology and Sociology, University of Virginia; "From Theology to Faith to Life Style" with Auxiliary Bishop William M. Cosgrove, Roman Catholic Diocese, Cleveland; "Clergy as Enablers of Personal and Social Change" with Bishop A. James Armstrong, Methodist Bishop of the Dakotas Area; "New Alternatives for Pastors and Parishes" with Reverend John E. Schramm, Community of Christ, Washington, D. C.; and "Theological Education as Process" with Dr. John C. Fletcher, Director, Inter-Met, Washington, D. C.

To those Academy participants whose contributions are included here, the editors are indebted. And to those whose material seemed not to fit the precise nature of this document, a debt is owed too; they share credit for the impetus which gave birth to this book, as do Professor J. Arthur Baird, founder of the Academy, and Father Elmer E. Marquard, its Administrative Dean. Dr. Edgar W. Mills and Professor Garry W. Hesser, Professor C. C. Goen, and Professor Rosemary R. Ruether have added contributions of note; we are grateful to them. For her cooperation and competence, our typist Marge Zimmerman deserves special thanks. Finally, and perhaps of most importance, the editors wish to express appreciation to the parish priests and pastors who participated in the Academy experience and who continue to reflect in their personal and institutional struggles both the confusion and hope of Christian ministry in these times.

G.R.B. and P.R.H.

.

I know all your ways; you are neither hot nor cold. How I
wish you were either hot or cold! But because you are lukewarm, neither hot nor cold, I will spit you out of my mouth.
. . . Hear, you who have ears to hear, what the Spirit says
to the churches!

Revelation 3:15–17, 22

Part One
The Confusion

Introduction

The crises crippling American Christianity, discussed in this book under the label "confusion," are primarily crises of identity. American churches—parishes, clergy, and laity—are indeed neither hot nor cold. Nor can they decide which they ought to be. Consequently, the churches flounder in a morass of indecision, either not knowing or else refusing to understand who they are and what they are called to be in the world. Not understanding their proper function as Christians in relationship to their culture, they too often do nothing in the face of a society in desperate need of healing. Feeling their identity threatened by change, American churches cling to traditions which have lost meaning or, alternatively, substitute gimmicks which equally lack meaning.

So long as churches remain lukewarm, they can be ignored with impunity by the culture. Those people who remain within the institutional framework will continue to make only minimal commitments. Critics will continue to level justifiable attacks against the contradictions and confusion, the ambiguities of purpose and action, which are the hallmarks of an institution no longer capable of recollecting its fundamental identity.

If the churches are to emerge from this period of confusion, they must rediscover and redefine their identity. The issues of role and function must be confronted—and acted upon. This process must begin at the parish level, for that is the primary unit of church structure. It is a process which must be participated in by both clergy and laity. Out of it must emerge functional new definitions of parish, clergy, and laity.

To begin the process both clergy and laity need to understand the confusion in which they find themselves. The chapters of Part One offer a variety of perspectives on the church which help to delineate the present position of the churches in society, to describe the relationships and interaction between clergy and laity within the parish, and to explain the historical process by which American Christianity has arrived at its present misunderstanding of its identity. Once the confusion—and the tangled and twisted thinking which produced it—is understood, the hard task of achieving a new sense of what it means to be Christian can proceed. Part One is designed to point out the confusion and to provide a basis for a continuing dialogue between clergy and laity on church renewal.

In considering the dilemmas which perplex American Christianity, it seemed important to first place the institutional church in a broad sociological perspective. Jeffrey K. Hadden's perceptive and challenging essay on "Religion, Inc." discusses ways in which the church functions—and malfunctions—as a social institution. Hadden clarifies the identity problems which divide churches and parishes, clergy and laity, without attempting to resolve them. Such a resolution must be worked out on the parish level through the mutual efforts of clergy and laity.

Edgar W. Mills and Garry W. Hesser in "A Contemporary Portrait of Clergymen" deal much more specifically with the internal functioning of the institutional church. Their particular concern is with the question of continuing education for clergy and with sources of clergy stress which have been incorporated structurally into the church. Understanding the position of parish ministers and the stresses to which they are subject ought to be a vital part of the continuing education of the laity—who, after all, are at least partially involved in creating stress and tension. The Mills–Hesser essay provides the laity with a basis for such an understanding.

The internal functioning of the church at the parish level is also the subject of Sidney D. Skirvin's analysis in "Christian Ministry in Earthen Vessels," although his perspective is that of theological educator rather than sociologist. His focus is on the function of the clergy and their needs and tensions, but his discussion of parish dynamics indicates the role of the laity in the joint ministry of the church to the world. Skirvin's emphasis is on the humanness of the church (i.e., the clergy and laity) which must be reconciled with its divine mission. In this context his concept of expressive purposes and instrumental means is useful for examining the church today and for constructing new parish models to implement the "servant" mission of the church.

In the concluding essay of Part One C. C. Goen traces the historical process by which American churches assumed a cultural definition. "The Cultural Captivity of the American Churches" bluntly assesses the contemporary role of churches within American culture. Goen contends that Americans have misunderstood the meaning of Christianity because they have allowed their culture to co-opt their religion and define it for them. In doing so they have come dangerously close to substituting civil religion for Christianity. Reexamining local parishes in the light of Goen's indictments makes the need for renewal painfully apparent.

The progression of essays included in Part One depicts clearly the confusion which plagues American churches today. Beginning with the broad sociological outlines, the successive essays sketch in the details of contradiction and ambiguity. The concluding essay, with its historical perspective, clarifies the process by which American Christianity reached its current crisis stage. Until the churches recognize their present condition, they cannot hope to construct a new awareness of Christian identity which revitalizes parishes.

> Our secular society is a fractured society that cannot find
> wholeness through the fractured ministry of a fractured
> church. We cannot come to be human alone. Why cannot
> clergy experiment with ways in which they can develop
> groups for mutual support and trust? Why can congregations
> not begin to learn the power of affirmation, and to sense and
> experience the strengths and healing that could come from
> an open and honest Christian community?
>
> CLYDE C. FRY
> *Clergyman*

1 Religion, Inc.

Jeffrey K. Hadden

Ours is a cross-pressured society. On the one hand we cry for
factual knowledge and hard data to make needed judgments about
everything from cholesterol intake to automobile models to the
people we employ in Washington. But on the other hand we decry
statistics, depersonalization, and computerization, the heritage of
the efficiency and technology our society joyously nurtured in the
early years of this century.

This paradox is particularly apparent in our attitude toward the
church. To view the institutional church as a giant corporate structure is to develop a plausible and potentially useful analogy. Yet
those who invest their time and resources in this corporate organization refuse to use available statistical data to inform their evalu-
ative decisions.

THE CORPORATE CHURCH

The church resembles a large corporation whose stockholders
read their annual reports and mask what they see with explana-

7

tions that the facts are not reflective of the true situation. Statistics, they say, mean nothing in terms of success. It matters little, then, that in 1959 this corporation made $51 million in profits, but in 1972 it lost $65 million. Profits declined from 1959 to 1965; the later years all recorded losses. In 1965 the expansion program peaked at $1.2 billion; in 1972 it was down to $800 million, actually a dollar value of only $480 million by 1965 standards of valuation.

No one seems able to accurately estimate the value of stock in this corporation. But while inside analysts argue persuasively that media accounts of decline mean little, other market analysts point to gloomy indicators. For example, in 1958 the corporation held 49% of the market, in 1972 it held 40%. A single large subsidiary held 74% of its market in 1958, but now can claim only 60%. No doubt these are still respectable figures, but competitors are gaining ground and the significant losses do not seem to be tapering off. Foreign subsidiaries are faring even worse. One European subsidiary claims only 3% of its market potential. Disagreement over comparing the domestic and foreign markets exists, of course, between those within and those outside the corporation.

A recent survey of stockbrokers reflects more interesting light on market potential. Seventy-five percent of those sampled felt the value of this stock would continue to decrease, while only 14% saw increase in the future. In a previous study in 1957, 69% of those sampled forecast increase.

Internally the corporation is also reflecting changes. In 1959, 88% of the management trainees completed their program and moved into managerial positions; by 1969 this figure was 57%. In the field a large proportion of recent trainees report they have been inadequately trained, that they have not been given the skills to implement company ideals. Job descriptions are ambiguous, role expectations are often incompatible, and directives from higher executives are often in conflict. Salary structures are also badly out of line with other corporations. At this time 32% of all managers (38% under 40) report they are seriously considering tendering their resignations. In addition to financial pressures job frustrations are most often cited as reasons for desiring to leave, while insufficient skills or overspecialization are pointed out as problems in seeking other employment. Overall, morale is quite low.

Management is also in conflict with stockholders. Many important stockholders profess absolute opposition to many managerial policies, but only the strongest pressure has any effect. Further, management itself is so split over policies there is intense disagreement as to what their products are and how to market them. Over the past decade a number of surveys have, as a matter of fact, indicated that from management all the way to the rank and file, half don't believe in their own product or feel committed to the goals of the corporation.

And meanwhile, back at the top, a large proportion of members of the board of directors deny there are any problems. Of the remainder some agree a few difficulties may exist, but these, they insist, are only minor and temporary; yet others see the declines as a sign of good health.

The picture here is grim. Faced with the data on this corporation, some persons with vested interests turn their heads from the problems and instead vent their emotions on those who call attention to factual information. It is as useless and wasteful to expend energy in this direction as it is to ignore the whole issue.

Corporate solutions are obviously not appropriate models for dealing with church problems, but the analogy between the church and a major business institution does hold to the point of a demand for corrective measures. It's an extremely complex and trying situation to face, but the church must confront its declining finances, membership and influence, or anticipate gradual demise. The horizon today offers no promise of a rainbow behind the clouds, let alone a pot of gold.

Its Future

In January 1973 the Dayton Family Foundation of Minneapolis sponsored a conference on the "Future of Religion." Approximately eighty of the nation's most prominent and influential church leaders gathered in Chicago for this thoroughly planned meeting. Reams of research and resource materials had been sent to each participant in preparation for discussion. Forty-seven church groups had been studied and case studies developed on each; members had been videotaped in discussions with their congregations or groups. Historian Martin Marty had prepared a summary of the social history of the church in America; Colin Williams, Dean of Yale Divinity School, had authored a theological perspective on the implications of the groups studied. There were also papers on the limits-of-growth controversy, as well as much statistical data on current trends in the church in America. All of this, exclusive of the videotapes, was circulated in advance of the conference.

This whole spectrum of information offered meager hope for the church. Not from a "secular social scientist," but from internal sources came unwhitewashed material; church problems sprawled across the pages.

And yet, amazingly, the church people at this conference gathered not in dismay but in celebration. In a turnabout reminiscent of the Wizard of Oz, the clouds became cyclones and we were catapulted into a church refreshed, refurbished, and renewed. We were expected to hold one hand to the communal, agrarian, escapist cults of Pentecostal Jesus Freaks and the other hand to the self-indulgent, mystical, personal growth groups, and trundle merrily along the yellow brick road to eternal bliss.

Such is the desperation of mainline, institutional religion. In the face of crucial social problems, the church leadership has followed the political leadership of our country and shrunk from its task. It has cowered before the implications of the gospel it preached on picket lines and grasped, instead, vulgar, self-indulgent expressions of Americana.

This is not to imply that the church had all the answers during the social activism of the 1960s. It is rather an assertion that the church was beginning to recognize an important mission and now has, instead, joined (or perhaps led) the ranks of those who, failing to see immediate changes, now see no problems. Escapism as seen in the Jesus Freak movement ought to embarrass the established church, and as seen in personal growth movements ought at least not cause celebration. Most of the latter cult is comfortable avoidance, not conscientious preparation.

Many of those who only a few years ago took great personal risks to tug the church into the battle for social justice now embrace the flimsiest fads and foibles of our culture. Perhaps the riders on the freedom train didn't really comprehend how long is the journey to the proposed destination. Perhaps some were really only sight-seeing, or didn't pack enough determination for the whole trip. A human problem, this. But that's hardly an excuse for an institutional bailing out which tickets few new riders to continue the journey. Navel-gazing will never christianize our suburban Christians, a worthy task suggested several years ago now. Nor will patronizing and applauding the youthful participation in Jesus Freak movements lead either adults or young people closer to defining the path to mature responsibility in an admittedly confused world. It is gross misuse of youthful optimism and vigor to support its channeling into fruitless, self-indulgent ends. It is also basically un-Christian.

During the entire week of the Chicago conference, I never once heard anyone mention the statistical materials submitted beforehand. Only Martin Marty's paper was even cited, and this in relation to his thought that American Protestantism has never replenished itself from within. The connection: when all these young people are through their fundamentalist stage, they will flock to the mainline Protestant pews and all will be wonderful.

The Problem

But let us consider Marty's thought, for it seems to me that liberal Protestantism's inability to replenish its membership from within is one of the most telling barometers of its failure. To alter an archaic, pie-in-the-sky conception of faith into a relevant tool in the here and now world, is an outstanding achievement of liberal Protestantism. The god of this faith is vitally concerned with this life and works through men to make it a better and more just existence for all. This is a marvelous concept. It's also a very radical idea, but unfortunately the clergy who have forged this theology have never succeeded in transmitting it to a large majority of their constituency. The evidence of this is abundant in a hundred or more social science studies done over the past twenty years. Those who sit in the pews are essentially no different in their attitudes toward principles of social justice, conceptions of brotherhood, laws and the like from those who never set foot in the church. Until evidence indicates that those inside the churches are more vitally committed to the Christian ideals of the gospels than is the man on the street, there is little to become excited about.

The message of God's compassionate concern for this world must be the highest priority on the agenda of church leaders. Mainline Protestantism of the twentieth century has failed to get this message across and a viable future demands wrestling with this problem. Anything less will result, I think, in the continuing demise of mainline religion's role and position in American society. Protestantism and post–Vatican II Catholicism must find their own salvation in baptism into the real world they embraced briefly, and in service of the radical God who gives a damn.

But how can we shape ourselves to meet the demands of the tasks we face? Most of us lack the spiritual commitment, the psychic strength, and the intellectual competence to muster ourselves to the battles we know must be waged. Deep down inside we all hear whispers of what our agenda ought really to be. In our soberest, most intimate moments with the self, we know. But mostly we don't dwell so deep in consciousness, and how could it be otherwise? The gross discrepancies between our real and ideal selves would shatter the ablest personality were it not for the human dynamics for coping with tensions and conflict. Social psychologists have known this and have described well the mechanisms we employ to temper dissonance.

Often we deny the validity of our own feelings and convince ourselves an over-vivid imagination is casting shadows larger than our real experience of awareness. Or else we deny the realities we had focused on and offer ourselves excuses of exaggeration or misinterpretation of data. Further, we may choose to simply avoid the "bad news" of information which would reinforce our inner perceptions, or even seek counter-evidence as consolation. Sometimes we look to "authorities" to tell us everything is fine: "I'm O.K., you're O.K.," and the world's going to be all right, too.

Then of course, by minimizing our own capabilities and viewing problems from a guppy-in-the-ocean perspective, we can offer ourselves another escape. Or else we can rationalize our activities as somehow being relevant to the problem-solving we ought to be about and avoid our own indictments of stop-gapping and wheel-spinning. Finally, naturally, in our world of busyness we can manage not to schedule the moments of intense reflection when we might hear an echo inside suggest another road, a different map to lead us to what we really feel is important and worthy.

Now certainly, all this is human, very human, very understandable. But not necessarily immutable. To take seriously the challenge of today's world is to engage in a most threatening enterprise. The awesomeness of the problems, the dangers of failure, the intensity of needed commitment; the time, the energy, the drudgery—frightening prospects.

AGENDA FOR CHANGE

The world needs the church and its moral leadership to push, pull, and shove us deep inside ourselves, and then out to the front lines. But the church cannot serve the world in this way until it resolves to carry out its mission to mankind, sans rationalizations and procrastinations. To do this it must put its own house in order and realistically appraise its objective conditions. There are at least three interrelated priorities on which church leaders must focus their attentions. First of all, the credibility of the church as a sober and wise spokesman on important moral issues badly needs strengthening. The past has witnessed too much reticence from mainline leadership concerning important moral questions, simultaneously with unrestrained vigor and rhetoric from those at the fringes of the church whose moral positions are often, at best, loose interpretations of the Christian message. Contradictory claims to divine wisdom on moral issues will continue. But skill, restraint in selecting issues, and strategic planning to neutralize conflicting claims can revitalize the image of the church as a focal point of moral wisdom.

The second priority must be the reversal of the growing gap between clergy and laity before church leaders find themselves standing alone, an island between two masses of laity, rather than serving as a bridge uniting for a better world. To consider the problem inevitable and insoluble is dangerous nonsense. Both laity who hold tight to orthodoxy and see their pastor as an apocalyptic Antichrist and those who feel all or most clergy are hopeless refugees from sixteenth-century molds, lost and helpless amidst the sophisticated dilemmas of the modern world, must be reached.

The former challenge religious leadership to creative endeavors to work with them and bring them along in the creation of a new moral order. Preaching at them will solve nothing and since they are theologically orthodox they are unlikely to drop out but likely instead to face and fight innovation. In the 1960s they fought by closing their wallets, and the pain was indeed felt since this group tends to include a large proportion of the more affluent. Alternatives are few: they must be brought to new expectations of what precisely the church is all about. Though change-oriented clergy shun this task as not central to their endeavors, there can be little doubt that success here would insure far greater effectiveness for the church in broader society.

Moreover, while church leaders ignore this problem, two very real dangers loom in the background. First, in what might be a rather simple coup, change-resistors might collectively use their resources to purge the church of innovative personnel. Second, and probably even more dangerous, lies the possibility of a massive defection from mainline religion smack into the waiting and welcoming tentacles of conservative religious groups with strong, right-wing, para-political leanings. This would deplete already scarce financial resources while swelling the ranks of a political alliance to neutralize, or perhaps overbalance, mainline Protestantism's efforts to effect social change. The forces of resistance would thus have won a major battle in defining the allegiance of God himself.

In addition to working with and winning over change-resistors, the church needs to pour energy into efforts to channel the talents of those who desire social change but lack the structure to make best use of their potential. In some instances this will mean reversing the church's image for persons who have already abandoned their religious affiliation in frustration. They need new hope, or better, evidence that the church is addressing itself to today's world. America abounds in people willing to give and to work, people not yet convinced that the ideals they hold for humanity are unattainable. If the church wills, there is a great, natural human resource pool waiting to be tapped.

These tasks cannot be underestimated in either their difficulty or their importance. And the third priority is no simpler: the church must develop a disciplined organization of highly skilled, change-oriented leaders. Although the decentralized organizational structure of the church presents severe difficulties for controlling input once professional roles are assumed, numerous possibilities for improving recruitment, training and socialization await exploration. Clearly, most seminaries require extensive curriculum revisions to prepare men in solid social theory and analysis of the political, economic, and social institutions of society. Practical politics of parish survival demand attention: the nitty-gritty how-to's for analyzing power, spotting change-seekers, tempering resistance, selecting personnel, augmenting ideas. If the church is going to have the kind of leadership it needs to effect change ten, twenty, or thirty years from now, courses in social theory and basic survival in the stained glass jungle must be given more than a token place in theological training programs.

Further, and equally urgent, is the demand for much stronger support mechanisms for clergy. Though Protestantism, as yet, faces less of a drop-out crisis than does Catholicism, the problems of morale and mobility are obvious. As Edgar Mills and his associates have described it, there are too few good jobs, archaic mechanisms for placing men in the most suitable situations, conflicting role expectations, and a variety of other problems which erode commitment and breed sinking morale. Mechanisms of on-going education and psychic support are urgently needed. If clergy should be expected to avoid hopping on bandwagons and proclaiming jubilation in Jesus Freak and other movements deleterious to the liberal Protestant goals of justice and brotherhood, they need assistance.

When the road gets rough, ministers too need outlets for their frustrations and reinforcement of their commitment. They too need to have the reassurance of their peers trudging along beside them that it's all really worth it. My own studies, however, indicate that little of this currently exists. Most denominations lack the resources and vision to create these mechanisms; most ministerial alliances, presbyteries, judicatories, and the like do not function in this way.

In all probability if this need is to be met, it will have to come as a grass roots movement. We know turned-on children are more effective in educating one another than highly trained professional teachers. We know people who have shared a common problem are more effective in helping one another than are outsiders. Why, then, shouldn't cadres of clergy join together in trust and commitment to help one another cope with the jobs to be done? Solutions are unlikely to come from on high. If, then, church bureaucracies cannot provide, clergy must follow the design of our founding fathers, who never expected much from their government, and do it themselves. Organize. Divide labor. Create reciprocal expectations. Utilize community resources. Build psychic support. Develop the collective strength to purge defense mechanisms and rationalizations, and get on with the work.

It won't be easy. But Winston Niles Rumfoord, the great historian of the war between Earth and Mars, put it most clearly when he said, "There is no reason why good cannot triumph as often as evil. The triumph of anything is a matter of organization. If there are such things as angels, I hope that they are organized along the lines of the Mafia."

> Too often the minister feels a sense of guilt regarding his
> qualifications to help others with problems he hasn't been
> able to solve for himself. Ministers need to realize that they
> cannot be self-sufficient. Sometimes the greatest help we can
> give others is in allowing others to help us. Our struggle for
> humanness must be a mutual ministry.
>
> LAURA NELL MORRIS
> *Minister's Wife*

2 A Contemporary Portrait of Clergymen

Edgar W. Mills
Garry W. Hesser

Analysts of the contemporary crisis of the institutional church
invariably conclude that creative leadership by the clergy is one of
the fundamental necessities to a resolution of the current problems. In the preceding chapter Jeffrey K. Hadden identifies the
clergy as the singular dependable resource for pulling together his
disintegrating "corporation." If professional ministers are indeed
crucial participants in the church's struggle for survival, then some
understanding of who clergymen are, what their professional problems are, and how they resolve their role crises is necessary.

The following chapter is a description and analysis of several of
the key factors affecting Protestant parish ministers. The portrait is
drawn from an extensive study which focused upon twenty-one
Protestant denominations.[1] The responses of approximately 5,000
clergy to a fifteen-page questionnaire provided a considerable

amount of information on continuing education and career stress points.

AN AGGREGATE PICTURE

The typical Protestant pastor is between 35 and 39 years of age, serves in a town populated by 2,500 to 49,999 people, was ordained between the ages of 25 and 29 (i.e., 10–14 years ago), and has never changed denominations. His father is likely to have been a farmer (24%), or a skilled laborer, or a foreman (20%). The parsonage also actively replenishes itself, with more than 12% of all pastors having clergy fathers.

Educationally speaking, 70% have at least a seminary education, with almost a third having pursued further graduate work. In addition, 15% have completed college, and two-thirds of these have had at least some seminary training. Nearly three-fourths of the ministers received their training in a seminary of their present denomination, with less than 7% attending nondenominational seminaries. Hence, one is left with the impression that the Protestant clergy both value education and secure it largely under the auspices of their own denominations.

Most of the clergy (84%) serve a single parish with a typical 1968 budget for local expenses under $20,000 (55%). The congregations they serve are characteristically a cross-section of professional, white-collar, and blue-collar workers. But this heterogeneity is not racial: 96% indicated that 90–100% of their members are white. Half the parishes are located in counties with a central city of 50,000 or more.

Quite often the Protestant clergyman has been in his present position less than five years (46%), although 34% have been in their current locations more than ten years. Over one-third were in their first or second pastorates.

Nearly half the clergy indicated that they "specialize" in some aspect of their work, "devoting an unusually large amount of time and energy" to this specialty. Most are full-time pastors, although 16% reported being involved in non-ministerial employment.

Married and living with their first spouse (93%), pastors typically have two or three children still dependent upon them, although 81% have no college dependents. About half the ministers' wives are employed, of whom 70% work primarily because their husbands' salaries are insufficient to meet family needs. The median total income from ministerial sources, including salary, housing, utilities, and fees was $8,037 in 1968.[2] There is considerable deviation, however, among denominations, with a range from $6,639 (Church of God, Anderson, Indiana) to $10,412 (Unitarian Universalist Association). In addition, regional variations range from $4,072 in the East South Central states to $8,726 in New England, with no regard for denominational affiliation.

Gross figures represent only part of an accurate appraisal of clergy compensation. Table 1 reveals how 4,984 ministers themselves perceive the relative "justice" of their economic rewards. In 1968 nearly three-fourths felt their salaries were too low in comparison to their personal and family needs, while 58% felt their salaries were too low in comparison to the work required of them. When ministers compared themselves to other comparably educated professionals, 87% felt underpaid. There is little reason to suggest that any adjustments have occurred to alter these attitudes. Even in relation to other clergy in their own denominations 42% believed their salaries were too low, and 59% felt that way in relation to their congregations. When asked how they felt about their own 1968 level of ministerial compensation in relation to some five standards of comparison, their answers, as can be seen in Table 1, revealed feelings of being relatively underpaid and indicated a strong current of relative deprivation.

SATISFACTION AND STRESS

Looking at satisfaction in the ministry and in specific pastorates, less than 9% were dissatisfied with "being in the ministry,"[3] but 16% were dissatisfied with the church they "now serve." About 14% indicated that they might not or would not enter the ministry if they "had it to do over." In terms of specific alternatives to continuing in their present pattern, 10% said they probably or

TABLE 1

Ministers' Assessment of Their Salary Level

In Relation To	Much Too Low	A Little Too Low	About Right	A Little High	Much Too High
Personal and family need	24%	47%	28%	1%	——
Work required of me . .	23	35	35	5	2
Other comparably educated professionals	58	29	12	1	——
Fellow clergy in my denomination	9	33	46	12	1
Living level of my congregation	17	42	38	4	——

definitely will leave the parish ministry (with an additional 36% open to such a career change), and 34% were either seeking or about to begin to seek a change of position.

The questionnaire included several items concerning current professional stress (defined as "situations which create serious problems for one's ministry"). The primary sources of stress were the need for more money and the work of the church seeming "futile or ineffectual."

The clergymen were also asked to recall earlier periods of major stress in their ministries. One-fifth mentioned three or more such periods. An additional one-fourth recalled two periods of major stress, and nearly another one-third reported at least one stressful time. More than two-thirds of these nearly 5,000 clergymen described their stress as severe.[4]

These findings were more recently corroborated in a Gallup poll (1971) which reported that one-third of the Protestant ministers and one-fourth of the Roman Catholic clergy that they interviewed had "seriously considered leaving the religious life."[5] Protestants attributed their frustrations to communication barriers with their congregations, inability to live on small wages, lack of interest and devotion of their church membership, irrelevancy of the church, and ambiguity of their role as clergymen. Communication problems with the parish, the desire to get married, the church's irrelevance, hierarchical rules and regulations, and the apathy of congregations were reasons Roman Catholics identified for seriously questioning their vocation. Age is a significant factor, the poll revealed, as nearly 40% of those under forty had "seriously considered leaving the religious life", while only 15% of the Roman Catholics over forty had entertained such questions.

DENOMINATIONAL VARIATIONS

Thus far the generalized statistics presented have tended to obscure the considerable variations in denominational profiles. For example, the proportion of ministers holding seminary degrees ranges from 11% to 97%, suggesting the difference between a church system in which access to ordained status has little association with education level and one in which educational standards virtually control access to the ministry. Another way to regard the data on seminary education is in terms of investment: in some denominations nearly all the ministers must invest the time, energy, and resources necessary to obtain a seminary degree, while in others this is not necessary, at least not through formal education. Investment may also be thought of in terms of years of service: ministers with fifteen years or more in the ministry have made a very high investment of their lives in this career, and denominations tend to differ by as much as seventeen percentage points in the proportion of their ordained clergy with such an investment.

Median income varies by nearly $4,000 among the twenty-one denominations surveyed, suggesting that denomination is a powerful determinant of salary level. Another quantitative indicator of the minister's position is the size of his local church budget, which indicates even better than the number of members the relative amount of resources available for use in the local church. In some denominations more than two-thirds of the congregations have local budgets under $20,000, while in others the proportion is just over one-third. These differences in available resources and clergy investment in their profession have been found to be significant in their effect on the behavior and attitudes of clergy, especially in relation to continuing education.[6]

CONTINUING EDUCATION

The questionnaire sent to clergymen sought information about four aspects of continuing professional education among ministers: the degree and type of felt need, the type and frequency of continuing education activity over a three year period, the obstacles to such activity reported by ministers, and the time and money resources designated by congregations for the ministers' continuing education.

Need was measured by using the statements and the scale shown in Table 2. The desire for continuing education was fairly evenly distributed, with two exceptions: "study to relate Christian faith to our rapidly changing society" was highly desired by 52%, while "preparation for another occupation" was highly desired by only 6%. The other five needs were rated high by 27% to 31% of the ministers. From 23% to 33% also rated these five low. It is worth noting that approximately one-third indicated little or no need for "learning how to be a change-agent in church and community," suggesting a potential, if not actual, polarity on this type of clergy role emphasis. In general, younger men tended to express greater need for each type of continuing education, with the widest spread being on the change-agent and skill-training items. Of the 4,984 respondents, 363 gave no reply to this series of questions.

The activity of clergy in continuing education shows greatest participation in institutes or seminars focused mainly on professional skills or on such subjects as theology, bible, and ethics, with organized reading programs third most often chosen. Fifty-seven percent of the clergy actually participated in some type of continuing education program in 1967/68, while 69% either participated or definitely planned to in 1969. The frequency of participation also differs somewhat. Twenty-nine percent of the ministers participated in one continuing education program in 1967/68, 16%

TABLE 2

Type and Degree of Need for Continuing Education

Type of Need	No Need					Much Need
Training in how to plan and evaluate church's work	14%	14%	23%	23%	10%	16%
Preparation for another occupation	78	7	5	4	2	4
Time to reflect on and evaluate direction of ministry	13	13	20	23	14	17
Training in ministerial skills (preaching, counseling)	10	14	23	23	16	14
Learning how to be a change-agent in church and community	22	12	17	20	15	14
Updating in biblical, theological, and related fields	11	14	21	23	17	15
Study to relate Christian faith to our rapidly changing society	7	8	14	19	24	28
Other (290 respondents added unique types not listed						

reported two programs, 8% reported three, and the remaining 5% participated in four or more.

Whether the ministers who participated the most are also those who reported the highest need is an important question to be dealt with later. It does appear that the institutional church is providing considerable opportunity for continued professional training but that a substantial percentage of the clergy were not yet involved at the time of the survey. In short, 43% had not participated during the preceding year of the survey and nearly one-third (31%) had no plans to do so in the immediate future.

This raises the likelihood that obstacles to participation play an important part in the continuing education picture. As might be expected, ministers identified time pressures (68%) and inadequate financial support (47%) as the greatest obstacles to their participation. Family pressures, unavailable programs, and resistant church boards were the other significant barriers cited by clergy. In addition to these external obstacles it is important to note two which are internal to the minister himself: "inability to read rapidly and with comprehension" (11%), and "lack of enthusiasm for continuing education" (10%).

The dominance of inadequate time and money as obstacles to continuing education activity is highlighted by the report of resources designated by congregations for their ministers' continued training. According to the respondents, the following allowances were specifically designated in 1969:

Time:	74%	none	Money:	80%	none
	7	1 week or less		6	up to $50
	12	up to 2 weeks		6	up to $100
	2	up to 3 weeks		2	up to $150
	2	up to 4 weeks		3	up to $200
	2	more than 1 month		3	more than $200

Three-fourths of the ministers have no time designated for continuing education leave, and four-fifths have no money allowance designated. Only 6% are allowed as much as $200, a relatively modest sum in the light of educational costs today.

Actual rates of participation in continuing education are partially explained by denominational affiliation. For example, 70% of the Friends and United Presbyterians participated in one or more types of continuing education. On the other hand, less than 50% of the American Baptist Convention, Church of God (Anderson, Indiana), Evangelical Free Church, Open Bible, or Southern Baptist pastors took part in any continued training programs during 1967/68. Furthermore, it is frequently the denominations with the highest levels of education that are also the leaders in continuing education participation, while those with lower basic education levels are generally lower in continuing education participation as well.

The similarly wide denominational variation with regard to time and money designated by congregations for continuing education each year suggests an obvious conclusion: that continuing education participation is closely related to the availability of time and money.

Clergy responses revealed further denominational diversity in the types of continuing education for which high need was expressed, in the continuing education actually done or planned, and in the types of obstacles to continuing education which were perceived. For example, the range of need for "training in how to plan and evaluate the church's work" went from 33% indicating a strong need (Southern Baptist) to 13% (Reformed Church in America). Nearly 10% of Episcopal clergy expressed a need for "preparation for another occupation," while in the Reformed Church in America less than 2% reported such needs. Some denominations fell below the national average on all items while others seemed consistently to be above or equal to the average on all the expressed need areas.

Similar diversity exists with regard to continuing education actually done or planned. For most denominations seminars in professional skills are the most often planned or participated in, with a few denominations emphasizing seminars in theology, bible, or ethics. Expressed high need for change-agent training and the number of seminars on social issues varied significantly by denomination, ranging from 4% to 50% and 10% to over 30%, respectively. These differences lead one to suspect that denominational subcultures, expressed in role expectations and norms of behavior for clergy, are a major key to the patterns of need and participation.

In spite of this denominational diversity, these variations do not appear to follow any consistent pattern with regard to theological position, type of church polity, or extent of clergy mobility. The more liberal denominations and more centralized polities did express slightly more general need, participate more frequently, and indicate a few more obstacles, but such differences were simply not statistically significant.

STRESS

Given this composite picture of the typical Protestant minister, it is important now to pursue some questions raised by the data regarding stress among clergy. Preceding any analytic efforts, however, must be a definition of stress. A useful three-level model of stress has been suggested in a study by Robert Scott and Alan Howard.[7] One type of stress is that which is deliberately induced, as in dangerous sports or training programs. Under these conditions stress functions as a positive factor. Another kind of stress is that which results from situations requiring an unusually high investment of energy to manage the situation. Scott and Howard label such conditions of continued but controlled high tension levels "first order stress." The final level is "second order stress," which is indicated when one is unable to solve or manage the problematic circumstances and begins to consider withdrawing from the situation. Stress, then, is a factor that can function in a variety of manners.

There are, of course, multiple behavioral responses that clergy can choose in coping with stress. Three possible responses and focuses of this study are those of leaving the local church ministry, seeking a new position, and participating in continuing education. The relationship between these actions and clergy experiencing stress is, not surprisingly, quite significant. The data showed a very strong association between stress and "seeking a new position" and an even stronger relationship between stress and anticipating "leaving the local church ministry."[8] Strong needs for continuing education were felt by those clergy with high levels of occupationally related stress.[9] However, in spite of the close relationship between stress and an expressed need for continuing education, there is very little indication that clergymen with higher reported stress actually have participated in or plan to engage in continuing education. These figures suggest the likelihood that substantial numbers of ministers in stress feel a need for continued training that they are unable to fulfill, which may possibly serve to increase their occupational stress.

One attractive hypothesis would explain "leaving the field"

(such as changing positions or planning to leave the parish ministry) as the result of having inadequate resources for obtaining needed continuing education to resolve severe stress. However, correlations of stress and leaving behavior in high and low conditions of need and resources are not consistent, and the highest correlation between occupational stress and seeking a new position[10] occurs under conditions of high money resources and moderate continuing education need. Responding to stress by leaving the field is thus not usually due to lack of continuing education resources.

In the range of alternative behavioral responses to stress, continuing education would seem to be one of the most constructive. It is clear from the data that certain topics of continuing education are more often desired by men undergoing stress, and that these may constitute viable alternatives to leaving the local church ministry, but once again participation levels are not closely correlated.

Our analysis has suggested thus far that one major factor motivating ministers either to leave the field or to feel needs for continuing education is the experience of stress. In an attempt to investigate further the stress condition, we tested certain possible structural and attitudinal sources of stress.

SOURCES OF STRESS

Our analysis suggests that several structural factors, including age, education, tenure, income, and congregational size, are somewhat associated with stress. Age seemed to be the strongest predictor of stress, whether viewed as the actual age of a person or his "career age" (the number of years in the ministry). There was a negative association of age and stress that indicated greater tendencies to report stress among younger or newer clergymen.

The overall findings coincide with a general theory of status inconsistency, viewed in terms of "investment" and "reward." In general the theory suggests that those who make high comparative investments (i.e., formal education and years of service) expect high comparative rewards (i.e., salary and church size). For our purposes clergy with inconsistent statuses have been defined as those who have either a seminary degree or fifteen years in the profession, or both, and who are below the average income, church size, or both. No implication is intended that ministers seek only or mainly material rewards, but rather that, in the church as else-where, people with above average years of education and service are not usually found in below average situations. Those who are so located rarely regard their situations as deserved but rather consider it something of a voluntary sacrifice, thus implicitly rec-ognizing that they occupy statuses which are inconsistent in the American occupational structure.

This measure of status inconsistency (or investment–reward inequity) proved to be only slightly associated with stress. Appar-ently severity of problems in the ministry is not related very closely to status inconsistency measured by objective indicators of age, education, salary, and church size.

However, when we look at more subjective indicators of *per-ceived* inequity, the association with stress doubles and triples. The results revealed three groups of subjective measures that are sub-stantially correlated with stress. The first comprises the minister's feeling about his own salary in relation to others'. The overall index of relative deprivation (based on salary comparisons with the standards listed in Table 1) is a relatively good predictor of occupational stress. And more specifically, feelings of inequitable pay in relation to congregation and other comparably educated professionals are even more predictive of reported occupational stress.[11]

The second subjective measure compares each individual's salary with his estimate of a minimum salary for someone with his investment of years as a clergyman. Stress is highly correlated with the situation of men with fifteen or more years of service who have a lower salary than they believe appropriate for that many years of service. For younger men, especially those without a seminary degree, receiving less than the appropriate salary appears to be much less associated with stress.

The third group of subjective measures shows the highest as-sociation with stress: satisfaction with the congregation being served and with being in the ministry.[12] It may be argued that stress and dissatisfaction are the same thing, but more likely they represent an overlap between a global judgment about ministry (satisfaction) and a series of accumulated feelings about specific ministerial problems (the stress items).

CONCLUSIONS AND SUGGESTIONS

From these data it can be concluded that status inconsistency can be considered a possible source of stress. However, the strongest predictor of stress is the subjective sense of relative deprivation or "injustice" with regard to salary. Moreover, while these relationships have been shown to be significantly high, it is impossible to identify any of these variables simply as cause or effect. Nevertheless, we consider status inconsistency to be both logically and temporally prior to stress level, and relative deprivation to be the result of conscious comparison with external standards, producing stressful feelings.

From this study it is clear that a significant number of clergymen experience severe stress. Alternative behavioral responses are often limited to leaving the ministry entirely or changing positions. Although large numbers of clergymen recognized continuing education as a possible behavioral response, this option does not appear to be open to or utilized by many of those reporting the highest levels of stress. Essentially the professional ministry and the religious institution have yet to create viable mechanisms to resolve stress problems within the parish ministry.

The purpose of this essay has been to raise a number of questions deriving from an extensive study of nearly 5,000 Protestant clergymen in twenty-one denominations. The focus has been upon a number of indicators of the overall morale of the religious professional with particular concern for occupational and general stress. Although many of the causes of stress among clergymen are no doubt idiosyncratic, psychological, and personal, our analysis clearly suggests that there are other potential, if not actual, causes of stress to be found in certain institutional inequities and situations that could and should be addressed by concerned church leaders, both lay and clergy.

In fact, it is precisely the stress-inducing situations caused by institutional paradoxes and inequities that are the most amenable to solution. The following article by Sidney Skirvin and subsequent chapters in this book explore some alternative mechanisms which could be helpful in the face of the issues and dilemmas raised by a close look at the clergymen themselves. It is precisely this type of exploration, positing of alternative mechanisms, and "thinking the unthinkable" that seems required in this era of the church's total ministry.[13]

NOTES

1. The study was conducted in 1968 under the auspices of the Ministry Studies Board, with the active cooperation of twenty-one denominations. For further details on the sample, the research design, and additional analysis see Edgar W. Mills and Garry W. Hesser, "Continuing Education and Occupational Stress among Protestant Clergy" (Richmond, Va.: Society for the Advancement of Continuing Education for Ministry, 1972) and Edgar W. Mills and Janet F. Morse, "Clergy Support in 1968," *Spectrum Journal* (National Council of Churches, Jan.–Feb. 1970).

2. There is evidence to suggest that this figure has increased in the intervening years, but largely in terms of a cost of living increment; cf. various denominational publications, e.g., "Pension Fund Newsletter" of Christian Church (Disciples of Christ), 1973.

3. Others might interpret this figure by saying: "Nearly ten percent were dissatisfied with being in the ministry. . . ." In other words, this figure may seem surprisingly high or low depending upon the perspective of the analyst.

4. See Edgar W. Mills and John P. Koval, "Stress in the Ministry," (Washington, D.C.: Ministry Studies Board, 1971) for a more extended report on previous and current stress and its management among both Protestant and Roman Catholic clergymen.

5. American Institute of Public Opinion Poll, conducted in February and March, 1971, with a total of 2,517 clergymen, including 1,192 Protestants, 845 Catholics, 421 Jews, and 59 of other faiths, as reported in the *Chicago Sun Times,* April 9–11, 1971.

6. For more detailed denominational comparisons see Mills and Hesser, "Stress among Clergy," and Mills and Morse, "Clergy Support."

7. Robert Scott and Alan Howard, "Models of Stress," in *Social Stress,* eds., Sol Levine and Norman Scotch (Chicago: Aldine, 1970), p. 259.

8. This assessment is based upon a statistical measure of association referred to as a "gamma." The gamma measures the strength of the association between two variables, i.e., the larger the gamma, the stronger the relationship. The gamma coefficient tells us by what percentage our power to predict one factor increases when we know the presence or absence of another. The gamma coefficient for "seeking a new position" was .43; for "leaving the local church ministry" was .54.

9. An occupational stress index was constructed from the five items related to the local church job listed in Table 1, gamma coefficient = .41.

10. Gamma coefficient = .61.

11. Respectively, the gamma measures of association were .31, .37, and .44.

12. Gamma coefficients = .55 and .63, respectively.

13. This chapter is a revision of an earlier document prepared for and circulated by the Society for the Advancement of Continuing Education for Ministry (SACEM). The authors wish to express their appreciation to SACEM and its executive secretary for their continued support, and to Charles Lindner who assisted in the preparation of this edited version of the original manuscript.

The primary site of theological education for clergy should be, and will increasingly be, the congregation and the community. This principle holds true for basic and continuing education. Every professional, insofar as possible, should be educated in the midst of the real pressures and decisions he or she will be facing, and every lay person should be involved in this process.

JOHN C. FLETCHER
Theological Educator

3 Christian Ministry in Earthen Vessels

Sidney D. Skirvin

Even marginal churchgoers can recall on command at least the essence if not the precise language of The Great Commission:

> Go, therefore, make disciples of all nations; baptise them in the name of the Father and of the Son and of the Holy Spirit, and teach them to observe all the commands I gave you. And know that I am with you always; yes, to the end of time.
> (Matt.28:19–20)

This was the theme around which Jesus of Nazareth called his disciples to a corporate purpose in the world. It is the task which the church continually has labored to fulfill. The charisma of Jesus motivated enthusiastic followers to share and to tell the "good news." Necessarily, then, the corporate group which boldly continues to identify itself as "Christ's Body" derived its reason for being from this Commission, and continues to do so.

THE PROBLEM WITH EARTHEN VESSELS

It is a long way from the noble intentions of this admonition, however, to the reports of contemporary critics about the church as a human institution—an earthen vessel of considerable fallibility. These reports should not have come unexpectedly. The account of the church's Day of Pentecost (Acts of the Apostles)—one wherein a new spirit enveloped the believers so that even as they spoke in different tongues, they could understand—is followed closely by a commentary on the lust for material possessions. People theoretically committed to a communal life style were discovered to be hoarding goods.

Nevertheless, some, mostly within the church, are still surprised and defensive about what the critics are saying: that the institutional church is full of the hypocrisy of endowment funds invested in the defense establishment, of million dollar sanctuaries in a country where people still starve, of self-righteous slogans and holy crusades of right and left which suggest no advance beyond the condition of the American body politic. The critics contend that the charisma of Jesus, so explicit in The Great Commission and implicit at Pentecost, has been routinized in an institution that reeks of establishment and creaks under the weight of denominational bureaucracies.

Lofty ideals such as the proclamation of Christ to the nations (Key '73) and the witness to peace on earth, and embarrassing realities like interdenominational bickering over the Consultation on Church Union and the church's refusal to urge amnesty for conscientious objectors against war: with these and other paradoxes the church lives out its struggle, guided by pastors whose very beings often reflect both the hope and despair of the church. The church, clergy and laity alike, must ask itself: can the church be different than it is? Should adherence to the spirit of Jesus produce a contemporary reformation which would strip the church of all its pious crust? Can it? Could the church return to the days in which "all things held in common" was a reality, to a time when those chosen by Jesus to be special disciples had a singleness of commitment?

Longing for such times and circumstances will not bring them about. For both pastor and parish, ministry occurs in and through earthen vessels, instruments of God burdened with human frailties. Like it or not, the church is the way it is—a very human, very fallible, very political institution. Its nature, with all the humanness apparent, confirms D. T. Niles's description of evangelism: one beggar telling another where to find bread. The purpose of this essay is to explore aspects of pastor—parish dynamics in an effort to assist both clergy and laity in understanding the frustrations and hopes of Christian ministry.

EXPRESSIVE PURPOSES AND INSTRUMENTAL MEANS

There are as many statements of the church's purpose as there are those who have risked the task of defining it. Theologian H. Richard Niebuhr succinctly described the purpose of the church as the increase of the love of God and neighbor.[1] Such an intention, hardly modest in design, is derived from The Great Commission. It is a process in which both pastor and congregation are to be engaged. One could say that "the increase of the love of God and neighbor" is the church's *expressive purpose*. It is the line which draws the church in all of its ambiguity to some degree of self-examination and self-transcendence.

But it is through the church as an institution, an organization, an "establishment" that this expressive purpose takes shape. In other words, the church employs *instrumental means* to establish its expressive purposes. The most prominent of these is the parish itself, one variety of which most Christians affiliate with, and one form of which most pastors serve. In a 1970 study of ministry, a research team of the Protestant Episcopal Church noted that "the parish will continue to be the unit through which most features of Christian life will be expressed for most Christians."[2]

Through this weak and fallible instrument, the parish, the church expresses its purpose of the increase of the love of God and neighbor. It dares to say that committee meetings, choir rehearsals, teas, weddings, receptions, funerals, worship services, counseling, letter writing on social issues, money counting, telephoning, and a myriad of other activities have at least the potential for being the instruments of God in the world of human affairs.

The church in the form of its varied parishes is a voluntary association. This is one of its instrumental characteristics. Few, with the exception of children and youth victimized by parental demand, associate because they have to do so. Reasons for voluntarily joining a particular parish are legion. Some, indeed, have come from north and south, east and west to sit at the table of the Lord together. That is, they see in parish life a slice of common humanity with which they want to identify in ministry and sharing. Others associate for reasons as diverse and diffuse as the parishioners themselves; far too often it is for reasons more social than religious. As the motives for parish membership vary and extend far beyond that singleness of purpose which characterized the early Christians, so the demands placed upon parish life multiply. Administrative matters take on increased importance and, as instrumental means, seem often to obscure the expressive purposes of the church. Both laity and clergy come to feel that the church's politics, created by virtue of its voluntary character, begin to contradict the church's purpose.

No doubt the clergy feel these contradictions most keenly, since they are by role more closely tied to the intersection of expressive purposes and instrumental means. When Samuel Blizzard published the first results of his study of ministry in 1956, he termed his article "The Minister's Dilemma." He discovered, among other things, that ministers generally felt least effective and enjoyed least the roles of organizer and administrator. Despite this, those interviewed said that almost two-fifths of their total workday was spent in administration. Preaching and pastoral concerns, the work considered most effective and enjoyable, was relegated to the limited remaining hours. For the professional, then, the expressive purposes may be obscured by the instrumental means in a manner not always apparent to the congregation.

These two concepts, expressive purpose and instrumental means, can assist both clergy and laity in understanding the dynamics of ministry. According to Niebuhr, the expressive purpose of the church is the increase of love of God and neighbor, whereas the instrumental means most visible are the parish and denominational support agencies for the parish. As a member of the parish congregation, or as the pastor, the question to which we have spoken is always present: can this voluntary association which we know as church legitimately function as an instrumental means for the expressive purpose of the church, given its human frailties, its inevitable though diversionary politics, its earthliness?

ROLES AND FUNCTIONS OF PASTOR

If one examines, within the framework of expressive purposes and instrumental means, the roles and functions fulfilled by the parish minister, the pastorate is exposed in a new way, to the edification of both laity and clergy. Whether we call this person the minister, the parson, the pastor, the priest, the teaching elder, or the enabler, he or she is involved intricately in the complex network of relationships which comprise the church. Though not necessarily desirable, the pastor, more than anyone else associated with the church, functions at the center of these networks. In the words of James Dittes, the pastor is "on the spot."[3] As the parish professional, this person stands at the point of intersection between expressive purposes and instrumental means.

What can we say about the pastor's roles and functions? In 1934, Mark A. May wrote concerning success in the ministry as viewed by laity and clergy:

> . . . There is no single secret of pastoral sucess. . . . But in every case it is a secret of fitting the pastor's personality, training, talents, and temperament to the types of problems that face his church and its people. In every case it is a type of adaptation different from any other. . . . Adaptation means, among other things, that the minister must speak a language that his people can understand; his church must offer a program of activities in which they can participate joyfully, purposefully and profitably. The aim of the successful pastor is not just to keep another church alive and going; to him the institution is only a means to an end. The end is to lead his people in the Christian way of life as he sees it, to help them with their personal problems, to educate them in Christian ethics, and to unify their total experience in an experience called worship. To this end, he uses whatever means may be at hand.[4]

If May is correct, then one of the ways in which to speak about clergy roles and functions is to see them in terms of the expressive purposes and instrumental means of which we have spoken. "Whatever means may be at hand" refers clearly to the instrumental nature of the parish, whereas to lead, to help, to educate, and to unify connote expressed purposes.

Later in the same study, May acknowledges the ambiguity of the "whatever means" when he says something that both pastors and congregations can surely affirm:

> What is the function of the minister in the modern community? The answer is that it is undefined. There is no agreement among denominational authorities, local officials, seminaries, professors, prominent laymen, ministers or educators as to what it is or should be. This lack of agreement, even along the most general lines, is a characteristic feature of the situation today and accounts in a large measure for the low educational status of the ministry. The work of the lawyer, the physician, the teacher, the artist, the writer and the engineer, is clear-cut and rather sharply defined (at least in the mind of the average man) so that when a young man chooses one of these professions he has some idea what he is getting into. But not so with the ministry. Entering the ministry is more like entering the army, where one never knows where he will land or live or what specific work he will be called upon to perform.[5]

In the nearly forty years since May wrote this analysis, history has passed by some of his remarks. More women are being ordained. Some of the professions to which he points are going through their own identity crises, as alert lawyers ask hard questions about justice delivery systems and social responsibility, as some physicians refuse to join the American Medical Association, as teachers form unions and go on strike, as professors find traditional classroom presentations challenged by restless students, and as engineers with high specializations are out of work.

Further, there is a crisis of authority in our contemporary American society that affects the clergyperson. In a recent article in the *New York Times*, James Reston noted that "there has been a sharp decline in respect for authority in the United States as a result of the war—a decline in respect not only for the civil authority of government but also for the moral authority of the schools, the universities, the press, the church and even the family."[6] Reston acknowledged publicly what we have all felt in our daily lives: the deep anxiety of a normless society which throws into question even the most established presuppositions and the meaning of human endeavor based upon those presuppositions. Inevitably, this crisis affects the church and its ministry.

Though written in the mid-1930s, May's comment about confusion regarding ministry still holds true. In the 1960s, James Kennedy described the ministry as an "octopus," with tentacles out everywhere.[7] The Blizzard study to which we have already referred, suggests that there are at least six roles the parish minister fulfills: preacher, pastor, priest, teacher, organizer, and administrator.[8] And to add to the confusion, this role diversity is set within the context of a very human, very diverse voluntary association which is part of a society undergoing the agony of normlessness.

The question, however, is a haunting one. In the midst of the diversity of ministerial roles in the parish, what is a useful (if not precise) definition of the function of the person who serves as the professional there? We have said already that this person stands at the intersection of the expressive purpose and instrumental means of the church. But there is also within the *life* of that person a similar kind of intersection. And the personal intersection, its character and shape, has much to do with effectiveness in ministry. For the pastor, expressive behavior includes the tasks of worshipping, preaching, counseling, and teaching, whereas instrumental behavior involves pastoral calls, administration, denominational activity, ecumenical activity, and community work.[9]

James Ashbrook has suggested that an "effective" minister is one "whose leader behavior combines in a more closely integrated manner an expressive awareness of people and an instrumental skillfulness in getting jobs done."[10] For James Glasse, President of Lancaster Theological Seminary, such an integration of expressive and instrumental behavior is best subsumed under the title, "pastoral director." This person is, in other words, a generalist, both willing and able to be sustained by the purposive vision of the

Expressive — worship, preaching, counseling, teaching.
Instrumental — Calling, administrating, denom. activity, comm. work. (?)

church and to express it. At the same time, he or she is committed to being an unabashed ecclesiastical politician for the sake of the instrumental means of the church.

Blizzard called the work of the generalist a "dilemma." Kennedy referred to its "octopus" quality. In a somewhat more celebrative tone, Dittes talked about the professional being "on the spot." Certainly within the generalist there is a dynamic tension between expressive behavior and instrumental behavior. Is this tension a dilemma? Is it a challenge to creative leadership in the church? Is it a destructive force which causes people to leave the ministry? The answer is yes to all of these questions. For this dynamic tension continues to be the determinant of pastoral roles and functions in the church. It is the power of this dynamic tension which causes some professionals to be perplexed, some to be enlivened, and some to move their ministry into other contexts.

THE PASTOR AS HUMAN VESSEL

In the foregoing section it has been suggested that both the pastor and his ministry are set at the center of conflict where the church's purposes and procedures are juxtaposed. Before indicating how the laity are implicated in and affected by this tension which, apart from the clergyperson, they feel as active participants in the life of the parish, it is important to speak of the pastor as a vessel of humanity. That is, the pastor does not enter the parish as a professional without a history. Aspects of his, or her life story relate directly to the choice of ministry as vocation, and the instrumental–versus–expressive tension arises long before professional ministry in the parish begins.

The process of entry into professional ministry usually begins in the home, the local congregation, the campus ministry, or in the classroom of a substantive college professor. Not surprisingly, people enter into training for ministry at least partially in response to a visible and viable role model, be that person a parent, a pastor, a campus leader, or a professor. It seems reasonable to assume that the major exposure a student receives from the professional role models he or she encounters in the parish is to the expressive side of professional behavior. The same phenomenon is

(& not the instrumental)

true, generally, with regard to a prospective pastor's campus involvements: the expressive side of a campus pastor or college professor is most visible and influential. Perhaps in rare instances persons are capable of experiencing the intersection of expressive with instrumental realities in those they emulate, but generally this is not the case.

As one moves from college to seminary education, he or she is thoroughly steeped in expressive behavior models. And seminary education does nothing to change that; in fact, it reinforces this pole of the dynamic tension we have been speaking about. Course offerings are in the fields of bible, theology, history, and practical theology. Ordinarily, the first three disciplines are seen to be functional for the expressive behavior of the professional leadership, particularly that of preaching and teaching. Since practical theology is regarded as the fourth field in seminary curricula, there is both a recognition of the importance of the instrumental behavior in professional leadership and a compartmentalization of this field. Hence, it is difficult for students and faculty alike to participate comfortably in the tension between expressive and instrumental behavior. Bible, theology, and history do not inform the political realities of seminary education and of the church as they should, and the political realities of parish life do not inform the classical disciplines. The difficulty which most seminary faculties have in integrating a curriculm is a paradigm of the work of the professional in ministry, but this is usually not shared in an educational manner.

Not surprisingly, the person engaged in study for professional ministry brings to it a well-developed personality, a life story. The profile of this story obviously affects in one way or another the tension between ministerial goals and means. In his book *Minister on the Spot*, James Dittes draws a hypothetical picture of a minister on the basis of a developmental model. His contention is that many ministers grew up as "little adults," more organized around the expectations of the adult world than the realities of their peer world. The adult values become the transcendent values for the peer world. The "little adult" lives in a world of peers while acting out the wide range of "oughts" and "shoulds" of a transcendent adult world. Dittes contends that the ministry becomes the rational extension of this role in life. The expressive behavior is most natural, allowing this person to be a "spokesman and custodian among . . . peers for the transcendent values."[11]

Even though Dittes is drawing a broadly sketched portrait of ministry, his insights are not without corroborative evidence. A recent study of the clients of a career development center for clergy indicated that fifty-four percent of the clients revealed themselves to be introverted personalities on the Myers–Briggs Type Indicator. Such personalities inhabit the world of concepts and ideas. For these persons, expressive behavior would be much more comfortable than instrumental behavior.

It is not difficult to understand part of what constitutes "the minister's dilemma" if one grasps what has just been said about pastoral roles and functions, on the one hand, and the psychological correlation of the life stories which many pastors bring to their professional ministries, on the other. In fact, it should be relatively easy for both pastor and congregation to comprehend some of the tensions which define their common life.

The church has both purpose and politics, and the theology which informs both is incarnational. God, indeed, works in the midst of ordinary people who live out their lives in ambiguous and petty ways. The clergy and laity are caught between the instrumental means and the expressive purposes of the church, though the former is obligated by profession to participate effectively in both aspects of the church's life. He or she is not only a generalist, but a generalist with a distinct tension in behavioral expectations. There is significant evidence to point to greater satisfaction for most ministers in expressive behavior. How the pastor and parish deal with these tensions will determine the success or failure of their joint ministries. The pastor must develop his own sense of self and mission as he deals with such tensions. However, as we shall now suggest, the laity have a clear role to play in the reduction of some of these dilemmas.

Parish Dynamics

It is not enough, in our examination of ministry, to speak only of the pastor's institutional and personal participation in parish life. To be sure, the pastor remains the focus of attention in church life, even though many would wish it otherwise. On the other hand, there are numerous examples of clergy who thrive on the authority and status they acquire via their professional roles. It is these persons who often lose sight both of the intention of a "ministry of the laity" and of the dynamics of parish life in which the laity plays a very significant part. It is through a partial explication of the latter that we hope to clarify the former.

Unlike many other institutions, the church has a unique set of client/employer/employee relationships which, far from being as irrelevant as they seem at first, have a direct effect upon its ministry and the roles of laity and clergy in it. In the church the clients and the employers are the same. Particularly in Protestant denominations, the laity are clients; they employ the minister to "serve" them. What this means for the pastor is that he or she is expected to meet directly the needs of those who employed him or her and who pay his or her salary. This economic dependency raises serious questions about the perimeters of one's ministry. In addition, the potential for increased conflict in this kind of system is obviously great; the multiplicity of expectations that can come from such a diverse set of client/employers is legion. Perhaps the first step in alleviating the negative aspects of this parish dynamic is for both pastor and parish to acknowledge its presence, to seek ways in which the pastor's economic dependency upon the parish can be reduced, and to view the congregation as a body called out for ministry rather than as a group of persons who have invested money in hopes of a pastoral return.

Closely associated with this relationship is another set of expectations placed upon the pastor and, more indirectly, upon the congregation. There are demands arising from the denominational hierarchy and from ecumenical programs. What the clients expect from their employee may conflict with what the denomination or the community expects. The same is true for the congregation. Its loyalty, too, is divided between pastor and denomination. At this cross-section of concerns, important questions inevitably arise. How autonomous is the congregation, the minister, and the individual lay person? What are the priorities in terms of sources of authority, by which the parish intends to organize its life? Do the pastor and the laity understand one another) on these matters? Though certainly no foolproof procedure for eliminating the tensions described above, these questions do indicate a place to begin. The questions are difficult; the fact that most parishes do not deal openly with them serves only to intensify adverse parish dynamics.

Another important dynamic of the parish, one related indirectly to those already mentioned, is the matter of ideological tension within the church. The social order in which contemporary Christians live and work is dynamic and complex; a church existing in it cannot but be affected by it. For many people, change within the society or the church is not a welcome event. It is a rational gesture for people confronted with change to hold on to what truths seem stable and still viable. Since the church has proclaimed its gospel to be just that, it should come as no surprise that it has as part of its constituency people who are both religiously and politically conservative. Yet on the other hand, there are those who, on the basis of hearing the same gospel, have been radicalized. Hence, ideological tension is a fact of church life which both clergy and laity must face.

As we have said, the church is an earthen vessel—a human institution which suffers from identical problems to those which plague all institutions. One of them is institutional sluggishness. About changing institutional life, one church sociologist has written: "Any naive assumption that one can easily affect and change complex systems is clearly in error. We should, of course, support policies which help to move institutions in directions we feel are important, but by definition policies within systems are interrelated complexly."[12] This has important implications for the laity. More than the clergyperson, the laity is the institution—financiers and therefore perpetuators of it. In and of itself, one cannot be critical of that. But when one puts together what the laity proclaims concerning the gospel, on the one hand, and the processes by which the institutional church functions, on the other, there is often room for criticism. Perhaps it might be suggested that the "ministry of the laity" could begin at home, so to speak; that is, with the processes and institutional structures through which the gospel is proclaimed in the local parish. To say this is to say the obvious: to the extent possible, the church's instrumental means must be made consistent with its expressive purposes.

A different matter of parish dynamics which relates directly to the laity has to do with the church's "theology of servanthood." Quite frankly, churchmen and churchwomen tend to use the model of servanthood as a pious catchphrase devoid of content. The words get filled with subjective interpretations, ranging from "doormat" to "unctious holiness." This tendency needs to be replaced by a different question: how can a theology of servanthood become embodied in the life of a parish, in the lives of individual laity, and in the life patterns of the clergy? With regard to the clergy some would argue that the terms "professional" and "servant" are mutually exclusive. Our contention is that a servant worth paying attention to in the church is one who has given serious attention to his or her strengths, abilities and beliefs, and one who knows with some degree of objectivity what he or she brings into the service of others. With regard both to the parish and to individual Christians, too often the matter of individual and corporate servanthood is not raised because all assume that the minister is to be the servant. Not only must the clergy begin to think seriously about the ministry of the laity, but so also must the laity itself. Those congregations employing clergy so that through their gifts they can vicariously participate in the Christian life as they watch the minister act it out have missed the point. Not only does the clergy not bring to the parish the kind of "supreme Deity, junior grade" which such a model suggests, but also congregations must discover at the theological level that the Christian life is not something to be discussed and observed, but rather to be practiced!

Finally, a rather mundane though hardly unimportant parish dynamic must be mentioned, for the laity play a large role in it. It has to do with support, emotional and psychological, for the clergy, as well as support, financial and material. With regard to the latter the known phenomenon of generally low salaries in the church needs little further comment. Numerous studies have shown that church professionals are among the lowest paid professionals in the United States. Certainly many of them make less than that earned by blue-collar workers. There is no philosophy or theology of wages, especially in the Protestant denominations. What does it mean to be an employee of the church, and a church employer? How does a theology of servanthood get translated into the realities of dollars and cents? What does it mean to take upon oneself a sacrificial way of life? These are not questions for only the clergy. The laity must ask them too, not only concerning their treatment of the minister, but with regard also to themselves.

Finally, the matter of emotional support for the clergyperson is central. Evidence is being accumulated to suggest that most clergy have no immediate and substantial psychological and emotional apparatus whereby they can derive support for their ministries. Pastors are highly autonomous individuals, due both to their own self-perceptions and to the expectations others place upon them. Hence, it would seem that no particular support systems for clergy are necessary. But precisely the opposite is the case. Clergy feel lonely, alone, and isolated. Though some semblance of discussion groups for clergy have begun to develop, it would seem that in this instance, the laity have an important ministry to fulfill. That is, clergy first of all need to be accepted as ordinary human beings devoid of all the professional trappings. And then they need to be incorporated into the sharings and strugglings that occur among the laity they have been called to serve.

By no means have the dynamics of parish life been exhausted in this brief account. Rather, the purpose has been to raise for the congregation some of the instrumental means of which they are very much a part and over which they have substantial control. In many ways the vitality of Christian ministry depends upon the partial resolution of some of these tense dynamics which affect laity and clergy alike. Though of a secondary, i.e., instrumental, nature, all are important in terms of a ministry that must occur within the parish before any authentic ministry can be extended by the parish and pastor to the world.

CONCLUSION

At the beginning of the 1960s, a decade during which much was written about the church and its ministry, James M. Gustafson published a book entitled *Treasure in Earthen Vessels*.[13] His important thesis was that those individuals and corporate groups engaged in Christian ministry ought never forget that they are human beings and that the ministry they carry out is identified with a human institution, a human community. This obvious fact, so it seems to this author, needs to be reemphasized today as the Christian church—or more accurately, the church struggling to be Christian—seeks to legitimize its presence in the world.

We have argued that if one employs the concepts, expressive purpose and instrumental means, it is possible to clarify in the life of an ordinary parish the issues with which both clergy and laity must deal. Because such confusion exists as these two realities intersect, it is important to understand how the church's purposes are constantly compromised by its instrumental means, and on the other hand, how means can be employed to augment the ends sought. More specifically, we have shown how the roles and functions of the pastor, and some of the dynamics of parish life, can be explicated via these concepts.

Christian ministry will always occur through earthen vessels: human beings and institutions. To eliminate human frailties is, obviously, not possible. What can be done is more modest and more profitable. Pastors and congregations can begin to probe into the internal dynamics of their common life together in an effort to understand what it is they are about. In that self-understanding, more truth and honesty about what it means to be the people of God in the world will prevail. And that is likely to provide increased self-awareness about individuals and institutions. If Christian ministry can begin to happen within the parish, then it is likely to happen beyond the parish in new and effective ways in the world.

NOTES

1. H. Richard Niebuhr, *The Purpose of the Church and Its Ministry* (New York: Harper & Row, 1956), p. 27.
2. Report of the Research Team Coordinating Committee, "Satisfaction and Dissatisfaction among Parish Priests: A Preliminary Discussion" (The Executive Council of the Episcopal Church, 1970), p. 2.

3. James E. Dittes, *Minister on the Spot* (Philadelphia: Pilgrim Press, 1970).

4. Mark A. May, *The Education of American Ministers* (New York: Institute of Social and Religious Research, 1934), 2:337–38.

5. Ibid., pp. 385 f.

6. The *New York Times*, 24 January 1973, pp. 1 and 17.

7. James W. Kennedy, *Minister's Shop Talk* (New York: Harper & Row, 1965), p. 104.

8. Samuel Blizzard, "The Minister's Dilemma," *The Christian Century*, 73, no. 17 (April 1956):508–10.

9. *Ministry Studies*, 1, no. 1 (May 1967):11.

10. Ibid. I am indebted to the research of James Ashbrook for calling my attention to the terms "instrumental" and "expressive," which he borrowed from the sociologist A. Etzioni.

11. Dittes, p. 134.

12. Thomas C. Campbell, "There Are Too Few Ex-Pastors," *The Christian Ministry*, 1, no. 6 (September 1970):21.

13. James M. Gustafson, *Treasure in Earthen Vessels* (New York: Harper and Brothers, 1961).

The church, its institutions, members, and clergy must take risks in order to be more in touch with the reality of the world. What is challenging is that the depth of that task to which we are commissioned is, like that of Jesus Christ, a risk of life itself. The risks are not being taken. The church is not distinguished in the culture as professing and acting out its Christianity. Neither are its members. That is the challenge of parish renewal.

DAVID L. BERKEY
Seminarian

4 The Cultural Captivity of the American Churches

C. C. Goen

Ever since the "surge of piety" in the late 1950s, critics of the church have been saluting (some would say assaulting) us with books like *The Suburban Captivity of the Churches, The Noise of Solemn Assemblies, The Stained-Glass Jungle, The Comfortable Pew, The Gathering Storm in the Churches,* and even *The Last Years of the Church.* Many such works, of course, are serious studies by responsible scholars; others are simply riding the crest of a fad. Some of the most penetrating critiques have come from unimpeachable friends of the church, engaged, as it were, in a sort of lover's quarrel. They were trying to be "honest to God" as well as to themselves, and the harsh things they said were spoken more in sorrow than in anger.

The underlying theme of most of these writers is that while American religion has never been stronger institutionally, it is scandalously weak as a force for moral transformation in the nation. In spite of the fact that nearly seventy percent of the American people are on the rolls of our many religious bodies, we are not at all the Christian nation we like to think we are but essentially a secular one. Our value system as a people derives not from the Christian gospel but from the general culture, i.e., secular society. The paradox, however, is that most church members (and many ecclesiocrats) do not know this, and if someone tells them, they do not believe it. Our churches are so comfortably domesticated in the American culture that they can operate with little sense of tension or contradiction between what they are doing as Christians and what they stand for as Americans. That is to say, our Christianity has been so accommodated to the prevailing culture that we have practically telescoped the mission of the church into the purposes of the nation. In such a situation the problem of identifying the church as People of God, the community of grace acting as his servant in the world, has become exceedingly difficult. This may become more apparent if we look at some patterns of our religious behavior.

LACK OF DISCIPLINE

One of the most obvious aspects of American religious life is the notable lack of discipline in the churches. Membership standards have almost disappeared, making scarce the obedience and devotion which define Christian discipleship in the biblical sense. According to reported statistics, we now have over 125 million members—for bragging purposes. We cannot begin to locate all of them. The leakage, in some cases, runs as high as thirty percent. Of those whom we can locate, we cannot count on more than half to be in public worship on any given Sunday morning. Of these "Sunday morning Christians" fewer than half will be active in the programs and organizations of the local congregation; and of those who are so active only a small fraction will be living disciplined lives of Christian obedience in home and office, market and factory, school and play. It may not be too much to say that authentic Christianity, in the sense of those who faithfully live out the meaning of their confession that "Jesus is Lord," has always been a minority movement. In any case, to use the name "Christian" for the undisciplined masses who are little more than practitioners of culture religion is to confuse the meaning of the term.

Anyone who doubts what I am saying should look at the reluctance of rank-and-file church members to seek a healing role amid the welter of moral crises which have been literally tearing apart the fabric of humanity in recent years. With distressingly few exceptions most churchgoers prefer the comfortable assurances of sentimental, privatized piety whose only prescription for a broken world is individual conversion to the same kind of piety. Whenever a community, whether a local neighborhood or the whole nation, is divided over some question with inescapable moral dimensions— e.g., race, welfare, peace, crime—church members rarely try to act on specifically Christian insights and seek a meaningful ministry of reconciliation. Instead they usually polarize themselves according to the conflict patterns which prevail in the wider society, thus reflecting the culture rather than attempting to bring it within the scope of God's judgment and grace. Ministers often think they have little choice but to acquiesce in this state of affairs, even if they personally would wish to do otherwise. Indeed, the localism and voluntaryism which have characterized American churches ever since their separation from the state practically guarantee that a minister will conform to his congregation's expectations and demands. Those who do not quickly find themselves in difficulty.

Suppose a pastor begins affirming that God loves the *world*, that Christ died for the *world*, that ministry has to be performed responsibly in the *world*—not solely in the safety of the sanctuary. Suppose he then engages in public actions that he feels express his conviction. I am not condoning all the bizarre behavior that has passed for Christian strategy in our troubled times; I am simply speaking of faithful ministers who, however limited their insights, try to witness to God's purpose that all men and women come to know themselves as his children and learn to live in his world as human persons in genuine community. If a pastor does this, the entirely predictable result is that many members of his congregation will respond with disapproval, dismay, and even hostility. The reason for this, I think, is that few lay persons have been taught to look upon God's world as the appropriate arena for fulfilling

Christian vocation. Hence the alienation between activist clergy and churchly pietists, or, as Jeffrey K. Hadden calls it in *The Gathering Storm in the Churches*, a "crisis of expectation." The average church member looks to his pastor for reassurance and comfort, to his church for identity and status, and to his hour in the sanctuary for a soothing religious nostrum. Some pastors, on the other hand, are impatient to give concrete expression to their faith. They feel, as Dag Hammarskjöld once put it, that "in our age the road to holiness necessarily passes through the world of action."

As never before in our history, the very structure of our success-oriented congregations practically assures that these divergent expectations will produce a ruction—if not open rupture. One pastor, out of seminary ten years and not about to quit, testified:

> For the past three years I have been pastor of a white middle-class church in a small city near Chicago. The congregation is strong, leadership adequate, and money available. But between the missionary potential of this congregation and the sea of human need around it stands an immense barrier, constructed of apathy, ignorance, fear, and outright hostility.[1]

And as everybody knows, many a sensitive minister has been turned out to pasture by pillars of the church who resented his active concern over such dehumanizing demons as racism and militarism. In short, when the crunch in the church comes between prophetic leadership and community consensus, a congregation's overwhelming impulse is usually to follow community consensus. Membership standards are virtually nonexistent, and demands for discipline get no hearing whatsoever. This seems to me irrefutable evidence of cultural accommodation, not obedient discipleship.

VAGUE FAITH

Another way of documenting this accommodation is to expose the vagueness of so many church members' faith—and by "faith" I mean the belief-structure which defines the classical Christian tradition. Hazy notions about God, aberrant ideas about Christ, fuzzy concepts of the church, vacuous verbiage about sin and grace—these and worse are commonplace. Without attempting to write a contemporary chapter for the history of heresy (which is admittedly difficult to define!), perhaps I can demonstrate the point by describing what has happened to the nature of faith itself. In 1955 Will Herberg, a Jewish sociologist of profound and prophetic insight, published an essay, *Protestant—Catholic—Jew*. The burden of that work was that Protestantism, Catholicism, and Judaism are no longer three ways of affirming something significant about God; they are simply three socially acceptable ways of being an American. That is to say, most Americans find their basic identity not as members of a company committed to a belief-structure and life-style characterized by a definite concept of God and what he requires of them, but as those who participate in The Amercian Way of Life. Martin E. Marty has described this phenomenon in *What Do We Believe? The Stance of Religion in America*, where one may read a good bit of data about a civic religious establishment which exploits the language and symbols of Judaeo-Christian faith so as to undergird the existing order. The God of America's *Kulturreligion* is neither the just and demanding Sovereign of the Old Testament prophets nor the transforming Presence who bound together the early Christians for faithful and loving service, but plainly a deification of The American Way of Life. This is what really defines their life-style, and as their ultimate commitment it becomes their religion. We may call it "the religion of democracy," "religion in general," or simply "the American religion."

The hallmark of this religion is called, loosely, faith. All of its high priests preach faith: faith is a good thing, everybody ought to have faith, only believe. The trouble with this is that nobody ever tells us what or whom we are to have faith in. Thus faith is emptied of content; it loses its object and becomes almost meaningless. It is simply faith in faith—which, being translated, means faith in ourselves and in our way of life. There was an outstanding example of this at the inauguration of 1968, when Richard M. Nixon became "the most publicly prayed-over new president in the history of the Republic." Curiously enough, after about the third of those five prayers (whose combined length was greater than the president's address) one got the impression that the purpose was not so much to humble ourselves before the Almighty but rather to recognize ritually that general religion is an integral part of American culture. But the emptiness of that religion became unmistakably clear in Mr. Nixon's inaugural speech itself, when he began to talk about our spiritual crisis:

> We have found ourselves rich in goods, but ragged in spirit; reaching with magnificent precision for the moon, but falling into raucous discord on earth. We are caught in war, wanting peace. We are torn by division, wanting unity. We see around us empty lives, wanting fulfillment. We see tasks that need doing, waiting for hands to do them. *To a crisis of the spirit, we need an answer of the spirit.* [Italics by C.C.G.]

So far, so good; and one waited expectantly for a prophetic explication of that "answer of the spirit." But in the next breath, without any interruption in the flow of oratory, the new president affirmed: "And to find that answer, we need only look within ourselves." There it is! The object of faith, so far as American faith has an object, is ourselves—the virtuous, hardworking, generous-hearted, successful pioneers and settlers who built this great country and are still its sturdy backbone. When the name of God is invoked in this context—and it often is—he usually comes across in the image of a white middle-class American. He may even judge "sin in general," but rarely does he judge *our* sins—specifically those of pride and prejudice, selfishness and apathy.[2]

The piety of the inauguration of 1968 was resolutely maintained, right down to the "God bless America" conclusion to the president's televised reaction to the Watergate scandals (April 30, 1973). The Official Family arranged for worship in the sanctified secularity of the White House under the ministrations of carefully selected clergymen, and it goes without saying that few of these court preachers ever spoke with the prophetic passion of a Nathan or a Micaiah (cf. II Sam. 12 and I Kings 22). Magnificent prayer breakfasts, thoughtfully open to reporters and photographers, have shown us our great ones with heads bowed and eyes closed, reminding us of the biblical injunction to pray in secret about as much as the menus of posh Washington hotels remind us of starving children in Southern shanties and urban ghettoes. But of course, it's un-American to starve in this land of unlimited opportunity for all, while to pray at public ceremonies is as American as cherry pie. Thus does so-called faith beguile us with the illusion of religiousness while concern for human beings goes practically unheard. To use the language of piety while flouting the summons to servanthood is to betray the extent of our captivity to culture and show how far that culture has shaped us in its own mold.

ONE-CLASS CONGREGATIONS

Another mark of our religious acculturation is the one-class character of most congregations. Whether one looks at the storefront church in the inner city, the exclusive temple with red doors out on silk-stocking row, or the modernistic hive of WASPs in typical suburbia, one sees in each case a group of people all drawn from the same socio-economic stratum. This, of course, reflects the character of the surrounding neighborhoods, and I certainly would not question the propriety of a local church ministering to its own geographical parish. But there are two caveats to be entered here. The first is that the pattern of residential segregation, reflecting the whole gamut of social stratification, delineates the deepest lines of division in our society today. So long as religious groups acquiesce in this state of affairs they are obstructing the will of God for human community. Ephesians 2 presents a breathtaking vision of the healing of our brokenness, which is surely God's ultimate purpose in redemption. John McKay once called that vision "God's Order," and I should like to believe that we can pursue it as a possibility of grace even in our disordered world. The only way we can do this is to think of the church as some kind of historical prefiguration of the eschatological community described in that superlative chapter of Holy Scripture. Unfortunately, that is next to impossible in our present one-class congregations.

Second, due to the reductionist ecclesiology which has long characterized American Christianity, we have succumbed to the temptation to think of the church as belonging to us: *our* church! Unconsciously we have come to feel that our church is for our class and kind; and what we like to call "fellowship" is really no more than social compatibility, not true Christian koinonia. When we are called to think of the church of God as truly embracing all kinds of persons from all stations of life, it is often more than we can manage. Thus whenever some strangers who are not our class and kind make their way by some chance to our doors, even with the best of good will we find it terribly difficult to open up our "fellowship" and genuinely include them. David Poling puts the point strongly in *The Last Years of the Church*, when he speaks of a "church that looks out upon the world with the appearance of a Federal Reserve Branch, staffed by uniformed guards who suspiciously peer at humanity from the safety of stained glass that is bulletproof, foolproof and compassionproof." But I suppose this is not too far from what we saw many times in the 1960s: ushers standing with locked arms on the church-house steps telling "outsiders" to get lost. Do not even the country clubs the same?

UTILITARIAN RELIGION

Another facet of American Christianity which ought to trouble us more than it does is what might be called the utilitarian function which religion is made to serve in our time. By this I mean that, whether consciously or not, many people tend to use religion to achieve goals which are not defined by religion itself. To speak of the desire of church members for status, comfort, and assurance is surely to sense the tension between this and faithful discipleship in the service of One whose ministry was that of suffering servanthood culminating in a cross. The church traditionally "glories in the cross," but if the present life-style of professing Christians is any evidence, this now means something far different from living under its demands.

There are many ways one might document this point, but I content myself with a few unoriginal remarks about one of the great high priests of utilitarian religion, Norman Vincent Peale. In the mid-1960s some of us were encouraged to think that Peale was quietly fading away from the American religious scene, but with the political ascendancy of Middle America he seems to have made something of a comeback. The same distortion, unfortunately, is still present—namely, that at bottom Pealism offers to teach people how to manipulate the principles of religious psychology so as to get what they want out of life. The joker is that what they want is not defined by the will of God as understood in any authentic religious tradition, but by the vulgar success philosophy of a materialistic age. Thus Peale and his disciples seem to be interested chiefly in how religion can help them to make money, lose weight, shoot a better game of golf, succeed in love, and in general, be happy. The way they often put it sounds very pious, to be sure, but at bottom it is religious utilitarianism, pure and simple: a man-centered, this-worldly, lift-yourself-by-your-own-bootstraps doctrine of self-help and selfishness. How could it be otherwise, given the vacuous faith I have described above? When one is unable to think theologically, to find a pattern of Christian thought by which to interpret the world and his place in it, the only sure thing he knows is his own self-interest. That is why Peale is so popular.

H. Richard Niebuhr once described movements like this in harsh but accurate words. He was speaking of Christian Science, but what he said applies with very little modification to the fundamental mood of Pealism:

> The development of this religious movement exhibits the complete enervation of a once virile faith through the influence of that part of the middle class which had grown soft in the luxury the earlier heroic discipline made possible by its vigorous . . . [self-denial]. Here the gospel of self-help has excluded all remnants of that belief in [Providence] which formed the foundation of Puritan heroism. Here the comfortable circumstances of an established economic class have simplified out of existence the problem of evil and have made possible the substitution for the mysterious will of the Sovereign of life and death and sin and salvation, the sweet benevolence of [an indulgent Deity]. Here the concern for self has been secularized to its last degree; the Puritan passion for perfection has become a seeking after the kingdom of . . . mental peace and [creature] comforts. This is . . . the religion of a bourgeoisie whose conflicts are over and which has passed into the quiet waters of assured income and established social standing.[3] [Brackets by C.C.G.]

So far as private piety is concerned, this seems to represent some kind of ultimate in cultural captivity.

THE NATION AS "CHURCH"

But there is a public manifestation of Christianity's acculturation in America, and it is perhaps the most disturbing of all. To compensate for our loss of unity and identity, our lack of discipline and purpose, we seem to have come to look upon the nation itself as in some sense our church.[4] The success of aggressively evangelistic churches has produced what Franklin H. Littell has called a "post-Constantinian" situation in the United States. That refers to the fact that after Constantine (the first Christian emperor, A.D. 312–337) established Christianity as the official religion of the Roman Empire, multitudes of erstwhile pagans began to stream into the church with little understanding of the Christian way and less commitment to it. The church thus faced a staggering task of administering the spiritual nurture and moral discipline which would bring these "baptized heathen" to some semblance of Christian obedience. That was the main problem of the medieval church: producing in their hordes of pagan converts an understanding of what Christian faith and discipleship were all about. The history of medieval Christendom indicates that the task was somewhat less than fulfilled.

The parallel with the U.S.A. is obvious. Although we have rejected state establishments of religion, we have accomplished practically the same result under our voluntary system, bringing vast numbers of new converts into our churches through the techniques of mass evangelism. It may sound a bit harsh to refer to our 125 million church members as "baptized heathen," but the points made above suggest that what we really have in this country is a deceptive veneer of religious terminology and cultic practice over what is still a deeply rooted secularism. And that secularism, so far as it assumes a quasi-religious stance, clearly takes the form of nationalism. A pastor in Kansas City discovered this when he noticed that the two flags in his sanctuary needed cleaning. He first sent only the Christian flag to the cleaners and was mildly surprised that during its absence nobody missed it. When it was returned, he sent the American flag to be cleaned, and on the very next Sunday several parishioners raised all kinds of indignant questions about its absence! The compulsion which many congregations feel to display the Stars and Stripes in their houses of worship underscores the extent to which religion willingly serves the purposes of the nation. I suppose this represents the lingering spirit of Teddy Roosevelt, who once exclaimed: "The clergyman who does not put the flag above his church had better close his church and keep it closed!" Any thoughtful Christian will see immediately that whenever loyalty to nation is placed above loyalty to God, the nation functionally becomes God—and that is what the prophets called idolatry.

Herman Kahn of the Hudson Institute has observed that most Americans of the broad middle class still believe in God and go to church "with reasonable frequency." Many polls confirm this, some reaching as high as ninety percent of the population who claim affiliation with some church or synagogue. But what clearly commands their ultimate loyalty is the nation, which they have invested with churchly attributes and functions. To understand this, consider the following operational attitudes:

(1) Americans think of historic destiny not in terms of something that used to be called the kingdom of God, but in terms of national purpose. To speak of the consummation of God's redemptive work as the reconciliation witnessed in the eschatological faith of the church is almost to talk in an unknown tongue. But to claim that God designs to bless America, and through her the world, is to be understood perfectly. There are problems here, though, even for the most patriotic Christian. For when national destiny can no longer be identified with winning the West, or enforcing the Monroe (or Nixon) Doctrine, or dominating the international scene, our frustration knows no bounds. One might argue that the deep malaise afflicting American life in the last decade is rooted in the fact that for the first time in our history we have confronted a situation that would not yield to American power or acquiesce in the notion of America as bearer of a special destiny for the whole world. We have not yet learned that nations are only temporal forms of organizing a people's historical existence, that nations rise

and fall, and that (according to the Judaeo-Christian tradition) God's ultimate purpose does not depend on any of them. In the absence of such understanding, our customary response to any external threat is to apply maximum force immediately, for we fear that somehow God will be dethroned if the United States does not get her way in the world. This is the same reaction one sees among primitive peoples, where the tribal deity is supposed to protect and preserve the tribe; when he does not, it is assumed that he can not, and he is vanquished along with his devotees. In such cases it is not the god but the tribe—or in our case, the nation— which is regarded as the bearer of historic destiny.

(2) Americans find their unity as a people not in relation to the unity of God and his work of healing described in Scripture, but in relation to the integrity of the nation. We *may* be Baptist or Methodist, Jewish or Catholic—consensus in religion is not a high priority—but we all *must* be good Americans. We are not much bothered by the fragmentation of religious bodies, and we can tolerate schism in the body of Christ so long as there are a few ecumaniacs around to keep us from entirely forgetting the problem. But secession from the nation we will never permit, even if we have to fight a fratricidal war to prevent it. (The Civil War, in the judgment of most historians, was fought mainly over the question of national union, not over the moral issue of slavery.) There are many church people who make a great cause of anti-communism, because that supposedly unites us against a common foe, and very few who recognize the morality of the peace movement, because that divides us in times of national emergency. Thus the politics of consensus within the framework of patriotic Americanism takes precedence over allegiance to the community formed historically by the confession that Jesus Christ is Lord.

(3) Americans view moral discipline no longer as the responsibility of the churches but as one of the functions of government. Some of the most virulent forms of racism, violence, lawlessness, and greed have been openly practiced by church members, some of them nationally prominent; and if one has ever been censured by his or her fellow Christians, the record has escaped me. What morality the country manages to maintain in its public life is due

more to the federal courts (which have provided the first line of defense against systemic racism), regulatory agencies (which attempt to limit the rapacity of corporate greed), congressional investigating committees (which sometimes concern themselves with the integrity of the political process), and the FBI (which is presumably our mainstay in the struggle against crime). Private agencies like the American Civil Liberties Union, Common Cause, and Public Citizen, along with various consumer organizations, have developed some leverage in certain areas of moral concern; but in spite of our habitual cynicism about politicians, the nation as a whole still looks mainly to the forces of government—and particularly the federal government—for the maintenance of moral standards and the regulation of citizens' behavior. Indeed, it may not be too much to suggest that J. Edgar Hoover, to judge from the eulogies at his funeral, was the great American saint in charge of preserving national morality.

These are problematic affirmations, however, and some careful sorting becomes necessary at this point. At present there seems to be a curious polarity among those who view the government as major arbiter of morals. On one hand are those urging the suppression of individual disturbers of law and order while ignoring the much more deeply rooted structures of prejudice and greed. Some of the congressmen, for example, who appear so prominently (and piously) at prayer breakfasts vote consistently against measures designed to help needy people, while filling all sorts of pork barrels for wealthy friends who keep them in office. On the other hand, so much needs to be done in the way of demolishing systems of legalized selfishness that some church people have been tempted to think that the kingdom can be hastened by means of social legislation. The clearest example of this is the series of civil rights acts passed in the 1960s: it is generally agreed that these could not have been enacted without consistent pressure from the churches.

I certainly supported this activity, doing my own little bit in preaching, lobbying, and demonstrating as the proper occasions presented themselves. But I continue to be troubled by the apparent disposition of politically active church leaders to think that the scandal which made civil rights laws necessary has been overcome.

That is to say, it is scandalous that in a land of 125 million church members, living under a democratic constitution, it still requires special legislative and judicial action to secure equal rights and opportunities for minority groups. But it is just as scandalous for people of unquestioned good will to think that the passage of laws or decrees of courts will do more than buy a little time in the present emergency. And unless that time is used for a redemptive ministry of reconciliation in the spirit of our Lord, our latter end will be worse than the first.

Let me illustrate by reference to our first Civil War. Long before the outbreak of armed conflict in 1861, many evangelical church leaders had regarded slavery as a moral issue to be dealt with under the demands of the gospel through the discipline of the churches. But this failed. Slavery was so inextricably a part of the Southern way of life, and economic considerations so compelling, that church leaders in the South joined the general chorus of support, defending "the peculiar institution" on biblical and moral grounds. (Utilitarian religion again!) When the moral crusade broke down, there was no recourse but to political action. Abolitionists viewed the churches as impotent; defenders of the slavocracy rejected churchly interference as improper, agreeing with Bishop John England of Charleston, S.C., that "when [slavery] can and ought to be abolished is a question for the legislature and not for me."[5] Thus the churches effectually abandoned their duty to condemn slavery as a sin and seek the moral rehabilitation of slaveholders. This was clear dereliction of Christian responsibility, fatal to the church as a socially redemptive institution and a crippling blow to genuine democracy. By relegating the question of slavery to the political arena, the church effectually surrendered its prophetic role as the transformer of society. Henceforth it would serve mainly as chaplain to those who practiced their piety in private and saw little relationship between Christianity and the social order.

We have come perilously close to the same stance today. What shall we think of a church when it has to call on the government to legislate morality on a higher level than it can achieve in its own membership by spiritual means? One may be grateful for con-

cerned clergy calling on Congress to act against fundamental inequities in our common life, but their voices have a somewhat
hollow ring in the absence of equally decisive action by concerned
congregations across the country. In the short breathing spell af-
forded by court decrees and social laws, we should remind ourselves that such things do not redeem, and continue to press the
quest for a truly human community rooted in Christian love. It
would be disastrous if we should prove content merely to rely on
civil rights laws rather than work to eradicate prejudice within the
church and reconcile our fractured neighborhoods in the spirit of
the cross—an enormously more difficult and costly task, by the
way.

One may reasonably conclude, in the light of these three operational attitudes (and more might be added), that the primary loyalty of most Americans is not to any specific form of the church
but to the secular nation, which is for them (in the apt phrase of
G. K. Chesterton) "a nation with the soul of a church." This is the
explanation, incidentally, for the great outcry in favor of religion
in the public schools, for in our kind of democracy the closest
thing we can have to an established church is the common school
system. When historic religious institutions fail in the ways I have
described above, we naturally look to other institutions to fulfill
their neglected tasks of spiritual nurture and moral instruction.
While many church leaders, to their credit, have vigorously opposed "Prayer Amendments" and similar misguided legislation,
popular opinion in the churches runs decisively the other way. For
most people, apparently, the public schools must be invested with
religious sanctions because they have the task of instilling the
values of democracy. In this frame of reference, democracy itself
becomes the national religion claiming our ultimate loyalty.

CIVIL RELIGION

So far I have been speaking mainly of the religion practiced by
the churches and how that religion has accommodated itself in so
many ways to American culture. Without turning entirely away
from that theme, it might be helpful now to shift the focus to
something called "civil religion," which exists alongside the reli-

gion of the churches. Civil religion is separable for purposes of analysis, but it clearly stands in strong symbiotic relationship with the churches' attitudes and practices. The term was popularized by sociologist Robert Bellah in an essay printed in *Daedalus*, Winter 1967. Since then there have been numerous discussions and debates over the phenomenon and its place in American life. Scholars have not been able to agree on a precise definition of civil religion, but I am not going to labor that point. On the functional level, it seems to me, it is possible to discern a kind of sanctified nationalism which may be called "the religion of the Republic," or simply the national faith. Such a faith is fairly elaborate, not only as the expression of general attitudes described in the previous section, but much more: civil religion in the United States is actually outfitted with all the institutions required by a living religion. Although not established in any formal sense by the law of the land, it is supported and perpetuated by the mores and folk practices of the American social mainstream. As a religion, therefore, the national faith seems to have its own seriousness and power. Consider the following aspects:

Ritual Occasions. Every religion must have its special occasions calling for ritual observance. For the American civil religion these are chiefly July 4, Memorial Day, Thanksgiving, presidential inaugurations, and perhaps the funerals of national leaders. These are not just holidays; they are holy days, traditionally celebrated with full religious rites intended to evoke the entire mystique of the American experience. Although they have no place in the calendar of any established religious tradition, they have long been sacred to every patriotic American.

Sacred Scriptures. The American holy writings, of course, are the Declaration of Independence, the Constitution, and the Bill of Rights. In a specially constructed building in the nation's capital the original autographs are guarded with as much care and reverence as any codex of Holy Writ. Streams of tourists pour through the National Archives, not to read but simply to look in awe. Copies of the sacred documents are printed in millions of textbooks; they are read at ritual occasions and honored in all quarters as the charter of our national existence. It matters not that sometimes they are conveniently ignored in practice—so is the

Bible. The point is that they are formally revered as the categorical imperatives of our life as a people, and thus they fulfill the function of sacred scriptures in the civil religion.

Myths and Symbols. Underlying the religious sense of American nationhood are major biblical archetypes: Exodus, Chosen People, Promised Land, New Jerusalem, Eden, Adam, Vicarious Sacrifice, and New Birth.[6] But the specific biblical content of these symbols has been evacuated and what stand in its place now are the events of the American experience. It was a commonplace of early American historiography to declare that just as the Hebrew nation was formed by its deliverance from Egyptian bondage, so the American nation was formed by deliverance from the British Pharaoh. And make no mistake about it: according to the national *Heilsgeschichte*, the last was an act of God as much as the first. Moreover, just as God chastened his earlier people when they were wayward, so he chastened his American Israel: the Civil War was a time of judgment.

In the heyday of the Second Awakening, Lyman Beecher had prophesied (1827):

> It [was] the design of heaven to establish a powerful nation in the full enjoyment of civil and religious liberty . . . to show the world by [a noble] experiment of what man is capable. . . . Is it too much to be hoped that God will accept our powerful instrumentality and make it effectual for the renovation of the world? . . . The light of [our] hemisphere shall go up to the heavens, it will throw its beams beyond the waves; it will shine into darkness there and be comprehended; it will awaken desire and hope and effort, and produce revolutions and overturnings, until the world is free.[7] [Brackets by C.C.G.]

Just as his puritan forebears had done, Beecher saw America as a city set on a hill, a light to the nations, an example that would save the world. But slavery was the awful bushel over the lamp of liberty. Slavery was the shameful sin of a people constituted by the declaration that all persons are created free and equal. Slavery was the hideous blotch on the escutcheon of a government that claimed to derive its just powers from the consent of the governed. And since slavery was not the sin of the South alone—Northern industry profited as much as Southern agriculture—the whole nation had to come under judgment. A generation after Beecher the gaunt man in the White House was trying to interpret for his countrymen:

> If God wills that [this war] continue until all the wealth piled by the bondman's 250 years of unrequited toil shall be sunk, and until every drop of blood drawn with the lash shall be paid by another drawn with the sword, as was said 3,000 years ago, so still it must be said, "The judgments of the Lord are true and righteous altogether."[8] [Brackets by C.C.G.]

Thus Revolution and Civil War, hope and judgment, birth and rebirth—these are the polarities of a history by which, as Americans believe, God has created and preserved their nation. It is this history which furnishes the myths and symbols of the national faith. They may carry the same names as their biblical archetypes, but it is the American experience which supplies their content.

Saints and Sinners. In the national pantheon George Washington is uniformly adulated as the new Moses—and Joshua too—who delivered his people from bondage and led them into the Promised Land of independence. It is almost impossible to exaggerate the reverential awe in which Washington was universally held down to recent times when acids of cynicism began to erode the romantic idealism of popular ideology. Listen to the paean of praise delivered in 1787 by Ezra Stiles, the learned president of Yale College:

> O WASHINGTON! how do I love thy name! how have I often adored and blessed thy God for creating and forming thee the great ornament of human kind! . . . The world and posterity will, with admiration, contemplate thy deliberate, cool, and stable judgment, thy virtues, thy valor and heroic achievements. . . . The sound of thy fame shall go out into all the earth, and extend to distant ages. . . . Such has been thy military wisdom in the struggles of this arduous conflict, such a noble rectitude . . . something is there so singularly glorious and venerable thrown by heaven about thee that not only does thy country love thee, but our very enemies stop

the madness of their fire in full volley, stop the illiberality of their slander at thy name, as if rebuked from heaven with a "touch not mine anointed, and do my HERO no harm." Thy fame is of sweeter perfume than Arabian spices in the gardens of Persia. A Baron de Steuben shall waft its fragrance to the Monarch of Prussia; a Marquis de la Fayette shall waft it to a far greater Monarch and diffuse thy renown throughout Europe; listening angels shall catch the odour, waft it to heaven, and perfume the universe![9]

George Washington is clearly the Superstar of the American national faith.

Abraham Lincoln has assumed the role of a Christ-figure among our "mystic chords of memory." He is the one who stood at the center of the nation's tragic struggle for cleansing and healing, and his death symbolizes the sacrifices by which the Union was reborn and redirected to its original purpose. If Washington is the "father" of the country and Lincoln the Christ-figure, it is tempting to look for a third person to complete the secular trinity. Here one must speak tentatively, but it may not be too farfetched to propose John F. Kennedy for such a role. The idea is suggested by the "eternal flame," a symbol of spiritual presence, which burns over his grave. Kennedy's historic place as a national leader is less clear than that of our other two "saints," of course, but myth-making need not be careful about historical reality. (Washington and Lincoln are being debunked by historians too, but this will probably not shake their places in the hearts of their countrymen.) In any case, the unprecedented outpouring of grief over Kennedy's death and the fact that his grave consistently attracts as many pilgrims as any other national shrine may indicate that he is being elevated into the upper echelons of the American pantheon.

The sinners and devils of American history need no extended comment. By definition they are all those, from Benedict Arnold to Daniel Ellsberg, who oppose what Middle America regards as the national purpose. Their presence over against the saints simply rounds out the observation that American nationalism has all the basic aspects of a religion. These aspects are fixed in the popular mind and sufficiently institutionalized to function as a coherent religion in the life of the nation.

There is a rather frightening aspect of civil religion, however, in the fact that it operates entirely within the parameters of American nationalism. When a nation like ours, with our history of pre-emption and expropriation, our sense of mission and destiny, our self-righteousness, and now our awesome military power—when such a nation comes to be accepted as "church" for most of its people, the possibilities can hardly be contemplated with equanimity. Who shall remind us, in the manner of Abraham Lincoln, of our finitude, our responsibilities, our inevitable call to give account of our stewardship? Apart from the rather remote and easily flouted provisions of the "sacred documents" cited above, there is no firm canon of judgment, nor is there any form of theism sturdy enough to undergird a doctrine of judgment and serve as a check to the idolatrous tendencies which develop. If the historic religious traditions do not assert their claims to ultimacy—and for the most part they do not—there is no witness to divine judgment anywhere. This tempts the national faith to become a sort of American Shinto, a formal state religion which could begin to require creedal endorsements of national policy. There is already ground for suspicion in the assertion that "the average American is like a child" who should obey his elders, in the fact that national leaders justify their policies by pious public relations devices rather than by honest information and rational argument, and in the vindictive use of such governmental agencies as the Internal Revenue Service to harass the "enemies" of the administration. In such a situation it is imperative that the historic religious communities be revitalized in a way that would enable them to challenge the pretensions of the state. As things are now, the symbiotic relationship between the churches and the sanctified nationalism that is the operating center of American civil religion seems practically to preclude a genuinely prophetic stance by the churches on any issue where it can be claimed that the national interest is at stake. The symbiosis thus becomes another link in the church's bondage to its culture.

HOPE

It is not widely recognized yet, but the United States is under judgment as never before. Failure to work our will in Southeast

Asia and the necessity to seek rapprochement with our traditional "enemies" have shown us that we are not as powerful as we thought we were. The uncertain status of the dollar and the awful realization that we are running out of natural resources—even the air we breathe—have shown us that we are not as wealthy as we thought we were. My Lai, Watergate, and other scandals too painful to admit have shown us that we are not as moral as we thought we were. Yet, as some rhetoricians are fond of saying, "crisis" means "dangerous opportunity." That is about where we are now, and I would argue that our case is far from hopeless.

We have heard our times called "post-Christian." That may be true for European society, though a more accurate term there would be "post-Christendom." For the United States, however, it would be both correct and hopeful to think of our society as being pre-Christian. As a matter of historical fact, this nation has never been Christian, despite a persistent myth to the contrary. When the United States gained its independence, fewer than seven percent of its people belonged voluntarily to any of the churches; and disestablishment of colonial state churches guaranteed that the voluntary system would become permanent. What members the churches have won, it now appears, have been persuaded largely by progressively reducing membership standards and the demands of discipleship. Thus Littell's analogy of the Roman Empire after Constantine becomes peculiarly appropriate: our millions of members with minimal understanding of historical Christianity urgently need instruction, and the fundamental task of the church today resolves into a gigantic one of Christian education.

I can be hopeful about such a task because of my faith in God, my belief that he continues to be active in the history of his people, and my conviction that the resources available to us are more than adequate for our need. In my humble judgment, this is a great day for prophetic preaching—notwithstanding the formidable forces that militate against it—and there are ways of doing this within the context of responsible pastoral care. This is a day for sweeping away the mists of a vague religiosity and exposing the vacuous pretensions of culture religion. This is a day for redefining the powerful symbols under which the people of God once marched in the obedience of faith. This is a day for developing informed and courageous communities of Christ who will demand of themselves and their leaders deeds of justice and mercy rather than ritualistic pieties.

The theological question with which we must wrestle over and over is always, How can the church become authentically the church? That question would require another essay—indeed, a lifetime of essays—but it may not be amiss to suggest a few tentative clues here. It seems to me that the church needs desperately to recover its identity as a community of vital faith whose fundamental shape arises out of its confession that Jesus Christ is Lord. When any other loyalty takes precedence over that ultimate allegiance, we are plainly idolaters. This means that we shall have to surrender the illusion of success through material growth, quit playing the numbers game, and reject the fatuous assumption that more means better. This is not to place any premium on smallness, but on faithfulness; and to trust God for whatever "results" he may grant to our obedience. If a congregation becomes serious about conforming its life to its confession, it will seek to be a community of reconciliation: reconciled to one another in such a way that the divisions which separate people in worldly society are overcome by their oneness in Christ, and reconciling through their witness and service in the world. Their worship will express their priesthood, as they bear the burden of the world's brokenness before the altar of divine grace, and their servanthood will seek to share with "strangers and aliens" the peace they have come to know in Christ. They will thus become a community of mission, seeing the whole world as embraced by the love of God, serving the needs of human beings in the spirit of Christ, setting all men and women free to become what God intended they should be.

Of all the symbols one might conjure with here, the one which for me is most pregnant with meaning is that of the Pilgrim Church. Read again Hebrews 11. Try to learn what it means to sit loose in the present and stay open to the future. See how the form of this world is always trying to capture the people of God and domesticate them in the present age, even though they know it is passing away. Discover the resources by which pilgrims of old pressed on in the obedience of faith, and why God was not ashamed to be called their God. Then make your own response to that disturbing conclusion: God has foreseen something better for us, that apart from us they should not be made perfect.

NOTES

1. Leon Sutch, "Essay on the Church," *Reflection*, January 1969, p. 5.

2. I am aware that the president's statement may possibly be taken as a reflection of his Quaker background. But it is scarcely necessary to judge the authenticity of that to know how his pronouncement was "heard" by most Americans.

3. H. Richard Niebuhr, *Social Sources of Denominationalism* (New York: Henry Holt & Co., 1929), p. 105.

4. Many of the ideas in this section were suggested by James E. Smylie's penetrating essay, "The Christian Church and the National Ethos," a pamphlet published by the Church Peace Mission in Washington, D.C., 1963.

5. H. Shelton Smith, et al., eds., *American Christianity: An Historical Interpretation with Representative Documents*, 2 vols. (New York: Scribners, 1960–63), 2, 201.

6. See Conrad Cherry, ed., *God's New Israel: Religious Interpretations of American Destiny* (Englewood Cliffs, N.J.: Prentice-Hall, 1971), pp. 1–30.

7. Lyman Beecher, "The Memory of Our Fathers," in Winthrop S. Hudson, ed., *Nationalism and Religion in America: Concepts of American Identity and Mission* (New York: Harper & Row, 1970), pp. 103–4.

8. Abraham Lincoln, "Second Inaugural Address," in Cherry, p. 196.

9. Ezra Stiles, "The United States Elevated to Glory and Honor," in Cherry, pp. 88–89.

When anyone is united to Christ, there is a new world; the old order has gone, and a new order has already begun. From first to last this has been the work of God.

II Corinthians 5:17–18

Part Two
The Hope

Introduction

To struggle through the "confusion" of Part One would be point-less if the despair did not somehow culminate in the "hope" of Part Two. The format used in this book reflects the basic premise that, despite the apparent despair concerning the churches, hope exists in the possibility of a new order in Christ. Even amidst the awareness of confusion, illogical hope—predicated on the grace of God—emerges.

Significantly, C. C. Goen entitled the last section of his essay simply "Hope." In it he suggested that compounding crisis may have the effect of precipitating change. Change, if implemented creatively, can become a source of renewal for the churches. It is his judgment that "the church needs desperately to recover its identity as a community of vital faith whose fundamental shape arises out of its confession that Jesus Christ is Lord."

It is to that need to discover an identity as a community of vital faith that Part Two speaks. The essays included in Part Two are intended to address the parish situation and to suggest to clergy and laity the directions in which the church must move to fulfill its mission of creating a new order and a new world. The essays themselves are designed to raise questions, to challenge assump-tions, and to reaffirm the applicability of the good news to the nineteen seventies and beyond.

In a loose sense, the four essays in Part Two parallel the essays of Part One. To accentuate the manner in which Part Two is a response to Part One, each essay in Part Two is preceded by a seminal quotation from the corresponding essay in Part One.

William M. Cosgrove's "Christianity: A Religion or a Way of Life?" poses the most basic question for Christians both as individuals and as parish communities: to what extent has their theology been translated into individual and corporate life-styles? Against the background of this basic discussion, he addresses the question of what it means to be the church at the parish level. To begin to deal with these questions in a serious and meaningful way is in itself the basis for hope. It is to begin to act upon the agenda which Jeffrey K. Hadden so correctly accuses Christians of ignoring.

The Mills–Hesser article dealt primarily with the clergy. A. James Armstrong's parallel essay, "The Word: Experienced, Incarnate, Enabled," also focuses on the clergy. In it, he describes the basic mechanisms operative in an effective ministry. The locus of hope identified in his essay lies in the possibility of an enabling ministry through which the Word can again function in the world.

John E. Schramm, in proposing a new modality for constructing parish communities, speaks directly to the conflict between expressive purposes and instrumental means which was fundamental to Sidney D. Skirvin's discussion of parish dynamics. "Parish as Christian Community" offers a resolution of clergy—laity tensions through the redefinition of that relationship in the context of a community. Schramm's conception of Christian community gives concrete form to the community of vital faith to which Goen alluded. His essay provides a basis for dialogue in parishes trying to move in positive directions toward renewal.

"The Believers' Church and Catholicity in the World Today" posits the global vision of messianic Christianity which Goen argues that American Christianity has lost in the narrow nationalism of civil religion. Rosemary R. Ruether's vision is that of the radical dreamer who refuses to accept the limitations imposed by cautious realists. Her vision of the new order reasserts the radical challenge of the Christian message. A Christian theology stripped of cushioning cultural assumptions is the center of the stark hope which can be discovered in the midst of crisis and confusion.

Confusion in the churches is a ground for hopelessness only when judged from the world's perspective. To accept the Christian perspective is to adopt a radical reorientation based on the paradox of hope which lies on the far side of despair. As clergy and laity begin to recover this vision on the parish level, as they begin to define and live out their corporate Christian identity, confusion in the churches will give way to a new order in Christ.

Most of us lack the spiritual commitment, the psychic
strength, and the intellectual competence to muster ourselves
to the battles we know must be waged. Deep down inside
we all hear whispers of what our agenda really ought to be.
In our soberest, most intimate moments with the self, we
know. But mostly, in our world of busyness, we can manage
not to schedule the moments of intense reflection when we
might hear an echo inside suggest another road, a different
map.

JEFFREY K. HADDEN
"Religion, Inc."

5 Christianity: A Religion or a Way of Life?

William M. Cosgrove

In the popular mind Christianity is understood as a religion, not a
life-style. It is considered, like Judaism and Islam among others, as
one of the major religions to which a significant segment of the
world's population adheres. That it is a way of living, and not a
religion, is what I want to insist upon and explain here. It is my
contention that theology, faith, and life-style cannot be separated;
that for those interested in vital Christianity, all three must be held
together in dynamic tension.

Let me explain, at the outset, that I approach this matter neither
as a theologian nor a scholar. I think of myself in terms of what I
am and what I do. That is, I am a street person, a parish priest, a
Roman Catholic Auxiliary Bishop. My recent involvements have
been in and with the parish: presently, with a black/white parish
on the East Side of Cleveland, Ohio. To incorporate these three

activities into one human life is not easy. The problem of trying to be a pastor and, at the same time, to handle chancery responsibilities as Auxiliary Bishop is a frustrating experience. Out of selfishness, some might say, I stay in the parish. They would be correct, for in the parish I can maintain my real ties with people. To be with a community of people and to share in their lives has been a source of great strength and joy for me in my priesthood. It is within this set of experiences, then, that I approach the question: "What is Christianity?"

A QUEST FOR LIFE-STYLE

It is in the parish, where Christianity is grass roots reality, that this question is being worked out by persons who continually try to understand what their religious commitment is all about. It is within the parish that we are constantly trying to integrate our lives as Christian clergy and laity with the urban community. On Cleveland's East Side, we do it through our grade school, through hospital work, through work with the aged and work with various community groups. Our task as Christians is to say to those who live in that community that we are there, that we intend to stay there, that we are interested in being there, and that we are there to offer support to them in every way possible. In other words, we are a Christian presence in that place.

To speak of Christian presence, of course, already suggests that Christianity is more than a religion. Rather, it is a way of being with people as their lives are lived out amidst the hurts and joys of this society. I am suggesting that if we are to be intentional about what we are trying to be, Christians in the world, then we must ask questions about our goals and our faith in light of the Christian message. We often fall short of these goals, but they are the end toward which we make a continuing effort in our work and lives. Unfortunately, the busyness of our lives often becomes an excuse for not taking time to examine and evaluate the consistency of our goals and of our life-styles.

For clergy, a periodic inventory to discover what we are is important. It assists us to grow as ministers in our appreciation of our roles. Indeed, one of the more hopeful notes of our times is that clergy are increasingly less content and complacent in their traditional roles. Hence, we are engaged in a constant search for deeper ways to appreciate and understand our relationship to Jesus Christ and to others in and through Him. We need to make certain that our life-styles actually reflect what we say we believe. This is extremely important if we are to be the effective presence of which we already spoke. Clergy of all denominations, I think, in this particular period of history, are trying to come to grips with this question of the consistency between theology and faith and life-style—this question of what it means to be an authentic Christian.

It is a question, of course, which laity as well as clergy need to ask. Let me suggest that it has a special urgency for the clergy. Within the church there is a great fear about hypocrisy, about being a phony in the faith. In some measure, this is a part of every Christian life. For the clergy this danger is compounded by the fact that, as a function of our roles, high expectations are placed upon us in terms of the integrity of our lives. We often find ourselves forced to masquerade, partly out of necessity and sometimes out of desire. We know we are weak human beings; yet we sometimes feel that we have a great responsibility never to show our weaknesses, or never to admit our weaknesses, or even to expect them in ourselves. It seems to me that these fears get in the road of our being able to develop and grow. We are not as willing to understand ourselves as we really should be. Then, when circumstances confront us with our humanness and our inadequacies, we feel compelled to label ourselves failures.

It is not surprising to find so many clergy today who are struggling with serious doubts about the ministry, or are even leaving the active ministry because they cannot reconcile their life-style with what they say they believe. For many, this is a period of confusion. My own view is that if we are to grow in our understanding of ministry, then we must confront and work through these doubts and the hard questions of how we accommodate our life-styles to our theologies. If Christianity is to be something other than a religion, then theology must be consistent with life-style, and vice versa.

Let me be more specific about my own concerns. I, too, am struggling with difficult questions about my own life-style, about my own ministry, about my faith. In my view, we need to share these struggles, both with our fellow clergy and our laity. From both groups we can find support and fortification. Christian ministry is everyone's calling, not just those who are ministers by profession. Because that work that we are called to do is so valuable, we must press on, despite the fact that we do not yet possess complete answers. We must learn to' live with our problems—or should I say, our humanness. And we can, if we understand ourselves and our relationships with others and with the Lord more fully. To reconcile theology, and faith, and life-style is not an event, but a continual process.

The problem of theology cannot be avoided in this process. What is it? For me, theology represents the science of faith; that systematic body of beliefs to which I have given intellectual assent. I submit that an understanding of theology is the basis of faith. For me faith is a deeper commitment to a body of belief than that of mere intellectual assent. The faith commitment of each Christian is the means by which he or she tries to live that theology to which he or she has given intellectual assent. There is only one way to make Christian belief active and vital: it is to live in such a way that one can experience the internalizing of belief in life.

Life-style, then, is the concrete and specific expression of that faith commitment. To say that one's life-style ought to reflect one's theology is to state the obvious. That statement remains an academic, intellectual abstraction until we proceed to use it to raise the more immediate questions which inevitably occur when we juxtapose our life-styles with our theology.

Some of these questions, oftentimes embarrassing ones, deserve our attention. We might ask whether, as we examine our Christian lives, both past and present, our life-styles really have been set apart from what we actually believe. Or perhaps we have claimed an inconsistency between our beliefs and our life-style in order to avoid the graver indictment that we are, in fact, truly living all that we believe.

What do I really believe? What one really believes, it seems, can only be discovered as one examines his or her life-style. In other words, what I say I believe is, ultimately, less a statement of my beliefs than the way I live. Words are cheap; it is very easy to give intellectual assent, to say I believe this or I believe that. But the only way I can know what I really believe is to examine how I am living. What my life-style is right now indicates what I really believe. My priorities of belief are apparent in my actions. How I understand the gospel must be measured by the degree to which I incorporate its message into my daily relationships.

It is very easy to turn ourselves and others off with pious words. We Christians, clergy and laity, can masquerade and hide behind our masks. But we really communicate our deepest commitments through what we live, and how we live. In fact, the way we live is the only way we can know what we believe. The only way I can recognize what really has captured my whole being insofar as the gospel is concerned is by seeing what part of it I have structured into my life-style.

To deal with such questions can be shattering, to be sure. The gap between the theology to which we have given intellectual assent and the actual beliefs reflected in our life-styles is immediately apparent, to ourselves and to others. This constitutes the hard reality, the basic discrepancy in our lives, which we try so hard to avoid facing. We don't want to ask these questions because we are afraid of the answers. So we postpone the analysis, promising ourselves that sometime soon we must go on a retreat to sort out our thinking and to catch up on ourselves. And then, somehow, we can never find the time; the busyness of our lives becomes an excuse. Clergy and laity in the parish too often wait to have their thinking done for them by the professional scholars and theologians. Questions of life-style are too important and too personal in their implications for us to avoid any longer. Each individual Christian, clergy or laity, must get to the issue of life-style, and ask himself and herself certain very, very, basic questions.

The answers to life-style questions must be measured carefully. From them we can determine the priorities that order our actions. Where do I spend my time? What do I do with my free time? If I have time just to think, what do I think about? When I have extra money, what do I do with it? The answers to questions like these must be measured against that to which we have given intellectual assent, against that to which we have especially committed ourselves in our ministries.

This list of questions is certainly not exhaustive. These that follow have occurred to me as I have attempted to examine my own life and ministry. What part does prayer play in my life? Am I really a man of prayer? How much time do I set aside for study? As a priest, how do I conceive the content of my sermons? What am I preaching about? Do I follow my people, lead them, or ignore them? Am I a slave to organizations and activities? Do I sincerely seek the advice and counsel of others? Whom am I most anxious to please? Whom am I most anxious to make friends with? How detached am I from material possessions? How do I react to those who disagree with me? Is my parish a serving community?

These are some of the significant questions for me. They address the specifics of my life as a pastor; the answers to each must be measured against the theological system to which I have made a faith commitment. What makes these questions so difficult is that where I find discrepancies, I must make decisions. I must ask myself in what way I will have to change my life-style in order that it reflect more faithfully the theology to which I have made a deep commitment.

REDEMPTIVE LOVE

As Christians examine their individual styles of life, they will encounter what they actually understand the Christian faith to be. I have shared some of the recurring questions with which I struggle at the practical level and with which I think the laity must wrestle. Because those queries continually challenge me to articulate my understanding of the gospel, it is important to share some of what that good news means to me.

I believe in the triune God. And I believe that one of my greatest opportunities and greatest duties is to develop the relationship with Father, Son and Holy Spirit. As one's relationship with God develops, one is better able to relate to other people. I am convinced that, as human beings, we are weak and imperfect; that our strength comes through unity with the triune God who is the bestower of grace. Put differently, I believe that what is fundamental to being a Christian is living a constant, continual yes to the offer of love made by God to man through the Son. I understand the commandments as a guide to assist me in imitating the Son in my own life-style. And I believe these commandments are summarized in the love of God and the love of neighbor. The basis for determining what is meant by love is the way in which the Father loved the Son, and the Son loved man and woman.

To develop a style of life that is in agreement with the essence of the gospel is to clarify what we mean by Christian love. Christians use the relationship of Father and Son to describe love. And when we speak of such love, we mean redemptive love. That, it seems, is the essence of the gospel.

The first question that a Christian asks himself or herself in a decision-making situation is: What response does the redemptive love of Christ require that I make at this time, in this place? The question is not: Is it going to cost me money? Is it going to hurt? What about my future? What about my old age? What about my neighborhood? What about my house? What about my job? The question is rather: What course of action would be most consistent with the type of redemptive love found in the gospel which I continually say I believe?

Redemptive love rarely means taking the comfortable and easy path. God's love was such that he showed his love by asking his Son to do the almost unbelievable. And then the Son asked of his apostles the same thing; and that is what is required of us as Christians. Jesus never said, "Cool it." He said, "Go forth." He lived out redemptive love in his own life and then admonished others, "Go thou and do likewise."

We Western Christians too often forget that moderation is a Greek, rather than a Christian, ideal. We make the mistake of trying to moderate the message of the gospel so that we can comfortably integrate it into our lives without upsetting them. We fail to understand that the gospel message demands a radical reordering of our priorities, a commitment to a completely new life-style.

Redemptive love is a creative force. In order to free that creative force to work in our own lives, we must first reorder our lives so that we are no longer our own first priority. This does not mean denigrating our own worth or our special talents. Rather, I am speaking of the paradox which lies at the heart of the gospel: those who would save their souls must first lose them.

Redemptive love is not a commodity which can be possessed. It is available only as it is shared with others and given away. For the clergy, this means that we must discourage the laity from being dependent upon us. Too often we use their dependency to nourish our own egos. We are afraid to let the laity go; to let them loose to do what they think needs to be done. Rather than encouraging them to turn to us clergy as the sole possessors of redemptive love, we must share it with them, and they with us, and we must then urge them to share that love with others.

To pursue this just a bit further: as clergy we tend to have an overdeveloped sense of responsibility. In fact, we are often weighted down by that responsibility. We are quite paternalistic in our fear that something might happen to our people. We want to protect them from every possible danger. This turns into a holding action. I think this indicates that we don't trust the laity as we should. Perhaps we are afraid that if good and evil are confronted, evil is always going to win out. Hence, we try not to expose our people to temptation or to evil. In the process we suffocate them; we suck the life out of them by protecting them. Instead of giving them the Word and the encouragement to go out and trust in the power of God, we ask them to place their trust in us. Once having put ourselves in this position, it is not surprising that we find it difficult to accept our own humanness and our own inadequacies.

A Christian Life-style

To speak of the need for consistency between theology, faith, and life-style, and about the questions of life-style and the theological significance of redemptive love requires that we be even more specific regarding what this means in daily life. Though the concerns of laity are somewhat different from those of the clergy, the following observations will be put in terms of my own personal struggles as a clergyman.

For us Catholics the role of minister is divided into three categories: priest, prophet, and king or servant. The role of the priest involves sacramental and liturgical responsibilities. The role of prophet includes teaching and evangelical duties. And the role of king or servant means ministering to the needs of the community.

In exercising these three roles, the minister is instrumental in developing three levels of Christian community—a praying, proclaiming, and serving community. The last is perhaps the hardest to achieve. Yet to really make the parish a serving community in the world is a responsibility which lies at the heart of the Christian ministry, for clergy and laity.

To be a praying, proclaiming, serving community is what it means to be the church. It is often less difficult to say what the church is not, than to say what it is. It is not a civilization, a culture, an organization, or a social class. Neither is it a morality for well-intentioned people. It isn't a system of moral laws. The church is not the bearer of the Christian religion. Rather, it is people who have said yes to the redemptive love of Christ and who are beginning to explore together their understanding of what it means to be a praying, proclaiming, and serving community.

Our concern with life-style needs to reflect a consideration of what styles of life will facilitate the development of such a community of faith. As a Roman Catholic priest, I have chosen a life-style structured around the religious laws of poverty, chastity and obedience. For me, these laws have attached to them specific and concrete life-style commitments. However, I am convinced that the spirit of poverty, the spirit of chastity, and the spirit of obedience have a far broader application as general characteristics of a Christian life-style. This is very important, it seems to me, for the laity to understand.

Chastity need not be understood as celibacy; it can also be understood as responsible sexuality. Obedience need not be understood as compliance with a specific set of rules, but rather as a maintenance of the self in a posture of openness to the guidance of the Spirit in sharing the redemptive love of Christ with and in the world. Poverty can mean the willingness to relegate material possessions to a role of secondary importance in our lives. More importantly, though, poverty can be understood as the spirit of humility—the lack of pride. It is this spirit of poverty which I consider the key issue. In significant portions of our society today, Christianity and Christians have become nonrelevant simply because of the pride associated with them—pride of social status, pride of race, pride of nationality. Until we can disassociate

ourselves and our faith from these types of pride, the Christian
faith will continue to be viewed as a white man's religion by minority groups. And it will ultimately be found meaningless by white
men themselves.

As clergy, it is our responsibility to take the leadership in our
own parishes in dealing with life-style questions. For ourselves and
our parishioners, we must raise them. All Christians, be they professional clergy or professing laity, must find—and live—a life-
style which is consistent with those beliefs to which they have
given intellectual assent.

Let me insist that by life-style I mean not so much a privatistic
daily scheduling problem as the way we relate to people through
our lives. It is how we go about building the Christian community.
For clergy it involves getting away from the privacy, away from
some of the separateness, some of the up-hereness, some of the I-
know-it-allness, to which we are so prone. It means really getting
on the street with our people so that we are praying with them; so
that we are not just talking to them, but are talking with them. I
think that as clergy, this is going to be our area of greatest adjust-
ment. We must break out of the paternalistic stance. We have to
build a serving community with our congregation. Our soul searching and meditation on our role as clergy must not become navel-
gazing. It must be shared with our congregations as a process in
which their participation is vital. Through this process we can
grow together so that as a parish we may become a serving community at work in the world, responding to the needs of the world
with a strength and an energy derived from our common life-style
based on the redemptive love of Christ.

CONCLUSION

Christianity is not so much a religion as a way of living. Unless
one's theology, one's faith, and one's way of living in the everyday
world are consistent, one's Christianity cannot be vital or meaningful. All three must form an integral unit which is then absorbed
into the manner in which we live out our struggles for humanness.
Ideally, such a Christian orientation will become so much a part of
who I am that it will be identical with my life. But this is not an

automatic process which is guaranteed to all those who are nominally Christian.

Most Christians have a way of life which they automatically identify with Christ's will for them. In fact, many have not thought at all seriously about how that way of living actually measures up to what Christian redemptive love is about. We need to take a step back from ourselves and ask the difficult questions: Does my present way of living reflect that which I believe most strongly? What are the demands and risks of the Christian faith which I claim to believe? What does it mean to make Christianity my way of living?

Today, I see people beginning to deal with these crucial questions, people groping their way toward a deeper understanding of some answers to these questions. I see definite signs of life. And I see signs of growth. I see more and more people praying together. I see priests with a greater desire to share themselves with their people and to lead their people in a spirit of serving. I have great hope of parishes becoming truly serving communities in the world as together we begin to live our faith.

It is clear that a significant number of clergymen experience severe stress. Alternative behavioral responses are often limited to leaving the ministry entirely or changing positions. . . . Essentially, the professional ministry and the religious institution have yet to create viable mechanisms to resolve stress problems within the parish ministry.

EDGAR W. MILLS and GARRY W. HESSER
"A Contemporary Portrait of Clergymen"

6 The Word: Experienced, Incarnate, Enabled

A. James Armstrong

Some years ago a major denomination assigned a priest to Indianapolis to be a minister to the power structure of the city. He came. He was given a list of the so-called movers and shakers of the city: businessmen, educators, political leaders. He dropped by my office one day, intoxicated with high hopes, to discuss strategy. How could he best enter the worlds of community leaders? How could he make the essential contacts? How could he provide those ministries that would help turn a city and its power structure around? We talked.

A few weeks later he returned to my office. The bubble had burst and he was deflated, disheartened. He had been received courteously by the so-called movers and shakers. They had greeted him; they had wished him well. But almost without exception each had said, "I have my own minister, you know." The priest's denomination had failed to understand, and the young man had failed to understand, that we are not simply assigned to tasks of strategic importance. We earn them. Over the long haul, through slow and painstaking efforts, we establish trust relationships and develop credibility. There is nothing automatic about the process and no ecclesiastical hierarchy can guarantee its success.

Let me suggest three essential approaches to meaningful involvement if as clergy we are to be *enablers*, in the process of making the church truly the servant of the world. One, we are called to proclaim the Word. Two, we are called to establish our own Christian identities in the world. And three, we are called upon to be available, ever mindful of who we are and whom we serve.

Proclamation: The Experienced Word

We are called to preach the Word as we understand and have experienced it. This does not mean that we simply put together traditional words that seem consistent with the faith. It means that on the basis of the authority of personal experience, we proclaim the Word. That is no easy thing to do in this moment of time. Our century has been a century riven and uncertain. Theologically we have moved from fad to fad and emphasis to emphasis. We have done the same ideologically, psychologically, and culturally.

Theologically we entered the century with high hopes, with the optimism of a promising social gospel. Then came the First World War, communist and nazi totalitarianism and a second world war. Reaction set in. The neoorthodoxy of Karl Barth and Emil Brunner became the vogue. Bultmann and Cullmann followed. Dietrich Bonhoeffer with his rigid Lutheran theology, his brilliant Christian humanism, and his courage and martyrdom inspired a generation of young Christian students. More recently we have seen a theology of revolution, a theology of liberation, black theology and a theology of hope emerge.

In psychology, as in theology, we have bent with prevailing winds. The names have been impressive: Freud, Jung, Adler, James, Coe, Pratt, Johnson, Wise, Rogers and all the rest. Divergent emphases have accompanied each new phase: pastoral counseling, group therapy, sexuality, human relations institutes, sensitivity training, transactional analysis.

Culture has shuddered on shifting sands as the high and naive optimism of 1900 has given way to the frightening cynicism of this current era of Vietnam, Watergate and a credibility gap that has become a canyon.

What is the church to do in the presence of changing winds and shifting sands? We have drawn from all of the contradictions within the various disciplines. We have been alarmed by headlines and responded to them. We have hopped, skipped, and jumped from one theological position to another, not realizing that we have become ideological pretzels in the process. We are faddists and dilettantes. We have spoken, yet our words have lost their meaning because the authority of personal experience, of real personal conviction, has been lost. Too often, our relationship to the gospel has degenerated into a stance uncertain, impersonal and academic.

In this moment of time, with many of us confused almost beyond our powers of endurance, it becomes supremely important for the church to speak a sure and certain Word. Within the limitations of our experience, but on the basis of our faith, we must proclaim a living and saving truth. The time has come for us to say, "We know whom we have believed!" And if we can't say that honestly, if He is not a part of our present experience, then as spokesmen for the church we need to search the deeps of our own beings. We have a Word to proclaim. *God is.* We may not be able to fully define. We may not be able to fully understand. But, *God is!* The Christian proclaims the nature of ultimate reality. He is Ground of Being, Creator, Sustainer, Spirit, Father; He is Love.

The reality of God is a part of the Word we proclaim. But this God is not an ethereal blur in the distant sky. He is not a theoretic abstraction. He is a participant in the ongoing experience of the race. This our Judeo-Christian faith insists upon. He is not a distant God, but One who works in and through the energies of the human community, helping give shape through instrumentality to all things that take shape.

The God of history has spoken through Jesus Christ. God was in Christ reconciling. The quality and power of his teachings, the beauty of his holiness, the profound depth of his sacrifice and the continuing ministry of his spirit provide the core content of the

Word we proclaim. In the grace of this gospel, old values and loyalties pass away and all things become new. We are "born again"—literally. We become new creatures in Christ Jesus.

But oh, the explosive ramifications of these all-too-brief and inadequate summary statements. Think where they lead. For, if God is love, if God is in history, if God has revealed himself through Christ, if life can be transformed, this is a Word that touches upon economic, political, racial and social justice; upon poverty, hunger, war and the liberation of humanity from its countless forms of bondage. When we talk like this we are not distorting the gospel. We are not adding our divisive notions to the gospel. We are proclaiming the gospel—the whole gospel.

Of course, there are risks involved; there is divisive content involved. We will doubtless be misunderstood and controversy will result. But has that not always been true when preaching has been faithful? In the Fifteenth Chapter of John, Jesus says, "The world hates you. Think nothing of it. It hated me first." In the Twelfth Chapter of Luke, he says, "I came not to bring peace but to bring division." He then goes on to describe those very generational and ideological polarities that are a part of our common lot today. Divisiveness, yes. Confusion, yes. Polarization, yes. But, faithful obedience is our calling and hope and joy.

We dare not take pride in controversy, nor dare we avoid it at all costs. Ernest Fremont Tittle is a name known to most. One of the truly great social prophets of the Christian faith through the first half of the twentieth century, he became in his later years more and more God-conscious. Yet he insisted upon relating that God-consciousness to a very real world. He was a pacifist, not only through the '20s or '30s, but through the Second World War. He applied the values of the gospel to the economic order and to racial tension. He served a "great" and affluent church, considered by many to be the "cathedral church" of Methodism. But because of his controversial viewpoints, the *Chicago Tribune* and the American Legion went after his scalp. Community leaders attacked his right to be true to himself. But his official board supported him and affirmed his freedom in the pulpit. (That from a well-to-do, reasonably conservative officialdom). Why? It was simply that prophetic as his voice was, courageous as his witness was, his love had been invested in his congregation, in all sorts of persons who trusted him and who would listen, in agreement and in disagreement, because they knew him; he had earned their respect.

At a time when the church is riddled with misunderstanding and suspicion we need to pause and reflect. Dr. Tittle knew that he was called to respond to the injunction, "Feed my sheep." No matter how pure the prophetic word or courageous the prophetic witness, if that dimension of compassion is missing, if love is not there, the act is shallow. We can have doctrinaire faith enough to shove mountains around, knowledge enough to get published in journals, heroics enough to have our bodies burned (or to withhold federal taxes), but if we don't have love, the rest is nothing. "Feed my sheep." What can I do, Lord? "Feed my sheep." Oh, come on, Lord. You know I do that. What can I do? "Feed my sheep." To pretend that the Word can be preached without a loving response to human need is nonsense.

But love is a two-way street. Insisting upon freedom of the pulpit, we must be equally insistent upon freedom of the pew. Only thus can we establish a climate in which mutual respect is operative. Messianism has been an unfortunate part of our ministries. The "Messiah complex" has hampered our effectiveness for two thousand years. But there is only one Messiah in the faith. I don't happen to be him, nor do you. With that firm knowledge, while standing unashamedly for what we believe, we can recognize that our awareness is not the whole truth. Even as we make our witness on the basis of the Word, we must be honest and human enough to recognize that there will be those who conscientiously disagree. Rather than be threatened by them we need to understand the pluralistic nature of the beloved community. Two of our Lord's disciples demonstrated that pluralism. Levi was employed by the Roman government. Simon the Zealot was pledged to the bloody overthrow of Rome. They sat side by side and found their unity in the Master's presence. In the face of divisive controversy we will learn the meaning of spiritual freedom. We will love. We will practice openness as a style of life.

The late Dean Miller of Harvard suggested that each of us should be a "disciplined amateur." We should not arrogantly pretend to know everything that is knowable, but we should be faithful students of the contemporary scene. What books have you read recently? What journals do you subscribe to, and what balance do they reflect? What are your study habits? What are your intellectual and spiritual disciplines? How does your congregation share in your growth? How broad a spectrum of reality are you exposing yourself to? The gospel of Jesus Christ is a "whole" gospel, related to all of life. We must maintain a balance that will nurture the community. The fundamental tenets of the faith must be related to social reality and our personal experience. The themes of faith and life must be brought together in the life of the parish. We are called to preach the Word on the basis of our own understanding and experience. It covers the whole realm of human activity and aspiration.

SERVANTHOOD: THE WORD INCARNATE

We are called to establish our distinctive Christian identities in the world. If we are to be enablers there must be more than proclamation. There must be demonstration, on the basis of our own personhood. We are called to function as authentic selves. We are persons who must somehow relate our personhood to the world around us.

In the Christian ministry we are not the "easy riders" of a counterculture, wandering from commune to commune, demonstration to demonstration, mission, as individually conceived, to mission, as individually conceived. We are members of a family, of a community. Within my particular denomination this is a community that is given form and definition by a *Book of Discipline*. Each of you has an equivalent network of earthbound definitions. We move under the disciplines of our particular orders and denominations. They are legitimate so long as they do not become the focus and substance of our calling. Beyond them, infinitely more important, is the fact that we are integral members of the Body of Christ. Joy on the part of one makes all joyous; suffering on the part of one brings tears to the eyes of all. Therefore, we cannot go off on our own individual ways; as Steinbeck's Casy said, "a-kickin' and a-draggin' and a-fightin'. A fella like that busts the holiness." Exactly so. We are in this thing together.

Dietrich Bonhoeffer was frightfully alone at the moment of his death, as every person is. But the fact remains that his last act before being taken to Flossenberg and his martyrdom was to lead a service of worship and share in Holy Communion. In the concentration camp he was spiritual confessor and acknowledged "saint in residence" because of the quality of his life. He died alone, yet not alone. His little book, *Life Together*, came out of the experience of the holocaust. In it he defined the nature of Christian "togetherness", of community.

Martin Luther King "did his own thing" as few men in our nation's history. No person in this century had a greater impact on the domestic scene. Yet he didn't do it alone. He was pastor of a Baptist church in Montgomery. He was co-pastor of a Baptist church in Atlanta. He had all kinds of questions about people like me, perfectly legitimate questions; and all kinds of searching judgments about churches like ours, perfectly legitimate judgments. He wasn't at all certain about the future of institutional Christianity as he experienced it. Beyond his reservations, however, the church was for him a reservoir of grace and good will. Nothing could take the place of the gospel songs, the camaraderie of the fellowship and the soul of the shared experience. He didn't do it alone. He relied on a community of faith and love.

Community is not only a Christian phenomenon. The An Quang Pagoda, the center of nationalist Buddhism in South Vietnam, was largely responsible for the demise of Diem's regime. The An Quang Buddhist monks stood together as they opposed the war, corruption, and a military police state. They brought the resources of their faith and life-styles to bear upon crucial need. They practiced self-immolation, not in isolated acts, but as members of community seeking to communicate.

We all have commitments. They may relate to liturgical reform or church renewal, to a resurgence of evangelical Christianity, the liberation of the Word, or to special ministries to the counterculture. These have their place, but they will be more effective if they are related to and emerge from the life of the church. We are called to be integral members of the body. If we are activists (and I commend the role to you) seeking to address ourselves to issues of poverty, corruption, drugs, war and oppression—issues that need to be analyzed in the light of the gospel—let's realize that it is far better to do so together than in isolated, Don Quixote fashion. Our commitment and servanthood should emerge from the collective context of a community of faith that gives added meaning to our lives.

Just as the individual must relate to the collective so should the collective concentrate on the individual. The individual is at the heart of the process. The servant activist who seeks to influence the course of events will be far more effective on the basis of what he is and does than on the basis of what he says. Ours is an incarnational faith. In a most profound sense, the Word will remain unspoken until it becomes flesh in us. Buddhists have been persecuted in South Vietnam since 1954 because of the nonviolent nationalism they insist upon living. Bonhoeffer was imprisoned and martyred by Heinrich Himmler because of what he had done. Martin Luther King received the Nobel peace prize, was consulted by lawmakers and presidents alike, was passionately loved and hated by his contemporaries, because of who he was and what he embodied. His widow, paying tribute to his ministry, wrote: "My husband healed more broken souls and bodies with his direct fighting message than thousands of his colleagues accomplished with pallid sermons addressed to half-empty pews."[1]

Community leadership will turn to us for counsel, not on the basis of an occasional race relations sermon or World Order Sunday pronouncement, but on the basis of our continuing involvement in community life; on the basis of our relationship to those problems and issues that are considered important by them.

AVAILABILITY: THE WORD ENABLED

How, then, can we develop a strategy of involvement? How can we be true enablers, influencing others? My answer is this: by *living what we believe and by being available to others on the basis of their needs.*

Do not delude yourselves. Rasputins and Richelieus are not in great demand. I doubt very much if John F. Kennedy had a "hot line" to Cardinal Cushing's office. The good cardinal played a significant role in the life of the Kennedy clan, but it was not linked with the formation of public policy. Richard Nixon is often photographed with Billy Graham. I doubt, however, if the president waits breathlessly for the evangelist's latest pronouncements on the depravity of man, the futility of social legislation, and the imminent return of Christ. Somehow these theological notions don't fit in with Mr. Nixon's—or any president's—"game plan." Presidents have their respected and qualified advisors. They also have their ecclesiastical acquaintances and "use" them in entirely different ways.

Some religious leaders have exercised significant influence over national events. Roger Williams anticipated our Bill of Rights. Benjamin Franklin was deeply moved by George Whitefield's preaching, though how he was moved—and to what end—we can't be sure. John Witherspoon signed the Declaration of Independence. The pronouncements and activities of clergymen were very much a part of the antislavery and temperance movements in the nineteenth century, and contributed to the mounting sentiment against war following the Treaty of Versailles. More recently, Reinhold Niebuhr and John C. Bennett have contributed to the formulation of national and foreign policy. And Cardinal Francis Spellman wielded a tragic influence over two American presidents and one secretary of state as Vietnam was split in two and the war in Southeast Asia unfolded. (Remember this: clerical influence is not necessarily divinely inspired!) Theodore Hesburgh is a Roman Catholic priest, as are the brothers and Fathers Berrigan. In most communities there are a handful of clergymen who are "with it." They are available to people, committed to justice, deeply involved with the issues, and are willing to take stands and run risks. And, believe me, the politicians know who they are.

For the past twelve or fifteen years I have considered myself an involved churchman. I have served on housing committees and worked with Model Cities programs; I have offered testimony at hearings in statehouses and in my nation's Capitol. I participated in the civil rights movement and have demonstrated for peace; I have been involved in reform politics at the municipal level, have served on state platform committees, and have introduced presidential candidates to assorted crowds of people during primary campaigns. I have signed petitions, written congressmen (and at least one vice-president), and have pled with friends to run for office and not to run for office; I have visited Cesar Chavez in California, Charles Evers in Mississippi, and Indian reservations in the Dakotas, as well as Paris and South Vietnam.

But again—we should not delude ourselves. Public officials are not on the lookout for self-styled, self-conscious "prophets of the Lord." If we are to stand by the sides of those called upon to lead their people in such an hour, we must earn our places with clarity of thought, decisive action, and a willingness to run the same risks and be judged by the same standards as other partisan activists.

Beyond such public participation, however, there is a more important ministry. Community leaders are human beings, often isolated and misunderstood, and they need the supportive care of the Christian community. Maybe this is what Norman Vincent Peale or Billy Graham brings to the Nixon household. Surely it is what Cardinal Cushing brought to the Kennedys as they faced tragedy and crisis together. Pastoral care provides the unique word and presence we have to offer.

As I remember the past decade of my own career, painfully aware of the controversies as well as the satisfactions, I am convinced that my pastoral ministry to public officials has been as authentic and effective as any other ministry I have offered. There was a time in Indianapolis when I was spending twenty-five hours a week in personal counseling. The problems were there to be dealt with: infidelity, drugs, marital strife, homosexuality, self-doubts, delusions of grandeur, alcoholism, realistic goal-seeking, serious illness, and deep disappointment.

In interacting with politicians and their families I have been confronted by exactly the same diet of personal and domestic crises. People in public life are persons, with all the faults and frailties, anxieties and bewilderments of any other members of a congregation. But they live in frightfully transparent worlds and are understandably reluctant to reveal their foibles and to share confidences. If we are called upon to counsel with them, their confidences must be fiercely and jealously guarded, as is true in all counseling. Such pastoral ministries are developed only on the bases of genuine understanding, demonstrated skills, and, most important of all, human trust. And lest we be carried away by our privileged status, we need to be reminded of both the wonder and the limitations of our functional roles. We are not analysts, secular therapists, or psychiatrists; we are servants of God seeking to fulfill our pastoral ministries. We must never lose sight of who we are and whom we serve.

The greatest gift we can offer any person (and this includes the politician as well as the day laborer) is an awareness of God's grace as revealed in Jesus Christ. As persons we can offer other things—friendship, opinions, counsel, and personal support. But God is the peculiar and unique resource we have to share. History belongs to him. Persons belong to him. It is our function to help bring them all together that the divine will might be done on earth as it is beyond.

I have been rereading the life of Gandhi. He was accused of being a saint who tried to be a politician. He corrected that by saying, "No, I am a politician who is trying to be a saint." On January 13, 1948, Gandhi began the last fast of his life. Five months earlier India had achieved her independence. Already violence was breaking out between the Muslim and the Hindu. Gandhi fasted to bring these enemies together. Sardar Patel and Prime Minister Nehru, dominant figures in India's government, were at sword's points. A part of the partition agreement creating a separate Pakistan, required 550 million rupees (about 125 million dollars) to go from the Indian treasury to Pakistan. Patel opposed the payment. The Prime Minister's cabinet agreed to withhold the money. Gandhi was in the third day of his fast when Nehru and Patel went to him to tell him about the action of the cabinet. Although Gandhi was not an official part of the government, he was the spirit of the New India. Government leaders knew they could take no major steps without taking him into their confidence. So they went to him, weak as he was, to explain their position. Nehru spoke, the Minister of Finance spoke, then Patel spoke; for more than an hour Patel developed his rationale. When he had finished, Gandhi wept and said, "Sardar, you are no longer the Sardar I knew."[2] That was all. The three men left and went back to the cabinet. The action was reconsidered and 125 million dollars was sent to Pakistan.

A bit more than two weeks later, Gandhi was shot and killed by a young Hindu fanatic. Lord Mountbatten hurried to the scene. When he arrived he found Patel and Nehru together. Tension between the two men had increased. Patel was convinced that the Hindus, that Nehru and Gandhi especially, had been much too easy on the Muslims. They came into the little room where their fallen leader was wrapped in a shroud of white, homespun cotton. Mountbatten said, "At my last interview with Gandhi he told me that his dearest wish was to bring about a reconciliation between the two of you."[3] The two men looked at one another, then at the lifeless form of Gandhi, and embraced. An essential unity was formed. The enabler was dead. Yet the quality of his life had been such that he brought about the greatest political miracle of modern history, the emancipation of a nation of more than 400 million souls. He embodied what he taught. Incarnational theology was at work in the life of a Hindu politician-saint.

We cannot be enablers unless we try to be what we talk about. We are called to reflect a distinctive quality of life in this world. Our lives, as nothing else, will provide the credentials we require. We must never lose sight of whose we are and whom we serve. Only as that identity is affirmed and celebrated can we be valid instruments in God's hands helping shape the present hour.

NOTES

1. Coretta Scott King, "The Legacy of Martin Luther King, Jr.," *Theology Today* 27, no. 2 (July 1970): 135.

2. Louis Fischer, *Life of Mahatma Gandhi* (New York: Harper & Row, 1950), p. 184.

3. Francis Robert Moraes, *Jawaharlal Nehru* (New York: Macmillan, 1956), pp. 347 f.

The expressive purpose of the church is the increase of love of God and neighbor, whereas the instrumental means most visible for the expression of this love is the parish. As a member of the parish congregation, or as the pastor, the question is always present: Can this voluntary association, which we know as church, legitimately function as an instrumental means for the expressive purpose of the church, given its human frailties, its inevitable though diversionary politics, its earthliness? How can a theology of servanthood become embodied in the life of a parish?

SIDNEY D. SKIRVIN
"Christian Ministry
in Earthen Vessels"

7 Parish as Christian Community

John E. Schramm

Saint Paul reminds us that being the church in the world means belonging to the community of Christ:

> Remember then your former condition . . . you were at that time separate from Christ, strangers to the community of Israel, outside God's covenants and the promise that goes with them. Your world was a world without hope and without God. (Eph. 2:11–12.)

His words mean being a covenant people, living out God's promises of hope amidst hopelessness. On the parish level the congregation is the visible witness to the world of what it means to be that community.

I am the pastor of an experimental ecumenical congregation in Washington, D. C. which calls itself the "Community of Christ." As we have struggled to understand what it means to be a Christian community, I have reached some conditional premises about what makes a Christian congregation a community of Christ, and about what the roles of a pastor and a group of laity ought to be within such a community.

Perhaps I will be forgiven if I say that I do not pretend to have anything new or startling to say. These reflections are matters we all know about, though sometimes we need to be reminded of them. Sometimes it helps if truth comes from someone who has had a different experience of it. When the experiences of basics occur in a different setting, they somehow seem fresh again. What I do not want to do is to make you wish you were in Washington, D. C. Nor do I want you to say with regard to the Community of Christ: "If only I were there with those kinds of people, then I could really function." That kind of projection is a trap. My conviction is that what I say can be appropriated to any parish setting.

Lanza del Vasto is the founder of a nonviolent Christian community in France. His books are now being published in English and therefore are available in America. Del Vasto visited Washington, D. C. recently and gave a series of lectures. In them he articulated three characteristics of a viable Christian community. They have been most helpful to me in structuring my thinking about experience in Christian community. Perhaps one could say they constitute a checklist against which we as participants in Christian congregations ought to measure ourselves and our life together. As I expand and define my thinking on community in relationship to these categories, I shall include a discussion on the role of an ordained clergyman or clergywoman within Christian community as defined by these essential functions. It will also become clear what I view as the role of the congregation in parish life.

A COMMON FAITH

A shared, common faith is the first characteristic of a Christian community. Theorists widely accept this notion; I believe, from the standpoint of experience, that it is a primary condition and essential foundation for any community.

Dr. Robert McAllister, a psychiatrist who lectured at the Liturgical Conference of 1968, spoke on "The Psychology of Community."[1] He defined an unhealthy community as one that had no boundaries. Such a community does not know what it believes, or that for which it stands. Without boundaries a Christian community cannot be viable; nor will it attract new members. Rather, those who participate in its collective meaninglessness will tend to drift apart because they remain confused about why they came together.

Faith has been articulated in different ways by different communities in diverse geographical and historical contexts. A common faith need not mean or imply unquestioning acceptance of any single, existent articulation of the Christian faith. Indeed, if a community's statement of faith is static, it runs the clear risk of becoming dogmatic tradition rather than the vital core of a specific congregational community. If a statement of common faith is to be meaningful in a unique congregational situation, and therefore a frame of reference that assists persons as they live out their daily lives, then it must be hammered out by that unique community of believers. Only the statement of faith which grows out of the shared life and understanding of the community can be considered legitimate by those in that community.)

Recently, a committee for the American Lutheran Church was assigned the task of working out new models for congregational life. That group came to an important decision. It recommended that no longer shall there be a "model constitution" for a new mission of the American Lutheran Church. The church will now begin to ask each individual group, as it seeks membership in the Church, to hammer out together a statement of its common faith. In my view that is a significant new step on the part of the denomination, and a valid approach. Each community must be able to articulate its own faith, else it will not know what its faith is. If a particular congregation has a constitution that is a valid expression of its life together, then it is indeed a fortunate congregation. Most congregations possess no such statement. In fact I know of only a few that have ever looked at their constitutions. And that is tragic, because Christian community begins with some basic premises about a shared faith, premises that must be shared in order to be real.

The Community of Christ has a covenant in lieu of a constitution. We have used the word "covenant" to remind ourselves that in Christ we are a covenant people; that we have become, in the words of Saint Paul, a part of the "community of Israel." Our covenant includes a strong affirmation of Jesus Christ as Lord. We have chosen to emphasize, as the source of our faith and life, the Christian understanding of grace, and as the norm, the Scriptures. The covenant invokes a relationship between members of the community which involves commitment to a specific Christian discipline of work, worship and study together. It lays stress upon the sacramental expression of our common life. The covenant is a renewal covenant; that is, it is reevaluated every six months so that recommitment is structured into our life together. Certainly this covenant as constitution is not the model other congregations should adopt automatically. Rather, this covenant faith is an example of what one Christian community understands as the vital center of its congregational life.

What is the particular role of the pastor with respect to this element of community which we have called a common faith? I want to submit that it is primarily one of *witness*. The pastor does not have as his or her primary duty that of being custodian of orthodoxy. Nor is he or she responsible for the faith of all those people in the parish. That would be impossible; it would also be a denial of the intention of community wherein all are ministers to one another. Primarily, the pastor is witness.

People, within or without the church, often sense phoniness instinctively. A pastor can be a faithful witness only to his or her own beliefs. Nothing is more empty than religious terminology which does not articulate a living faith. The primary function of the pastor, let me reiterate, is to witness to his or her faith. It is to first pray, and then give a course on the life of prayer. It is to believe before teaching theology.

If a pastor functions as a custodian of orthodoxy, he or she will find pastoral authority threatened by those who hold different beliefs and values. The authentic pastoral role is difficult because it has a maximum of authority, yet simultaneously is the opposite of authoritarianism. This matter of authority is crucial in dealing with the need for expression of a common faith. The custodian-of-orthodoxy role makes an authority conflict inevitable and it pushes the pastor into an authoritarian stance. If we can begin to think, rather, of the pastoral role as witness, the authority issue resolves itself. The pastor is left free to relate to people, and is freed to make his or her own proclamation of living faith.

Permit me to end this discussion of a common faith with one caution. Because a pastor is called to be a witness within the Christian community, and among its members, this does not absolve the community from the responsibility of being witnesses, too. Indeed, unless the community is in itself a witness to its common faith, individual and corporate, that commonality of faith has little meaning.

A WAY TO CELEBRATE

The second characteristic of a healthy Christian community is that its members have a way to celebrate their faith corporately. Sunday morning worship, in my view, falls far short of satisfying this essential characteristic. When I say that a congregation or a community has to develop a way to celebrate, I mean that, in some authentic ways, the life of that community must be shared and articulated in corporate expressions at different times. Births are an occasion for celebration. Baptisms must not be relegated to sometime on Sunday afternoon when only parents will be present. Funerals are not an isolated family affair at a funeral parlor. The sickness and joy so integrally a part of individuals' lives calls forth acts of community celebration and sharing. If Christian faith is to be a living, vital encounter with other persons and God, then these very human and very sacred experiences are essential to the living out of it.

In order to understand and appreciate celebration, "worship" needs to be defined and explained. Worship, in my view, is corporate celebration in response to God's grace, expressing the common life of the community. If one accepts that definition, then some false notions of worship must be abandoned. That corporate worship is the primary function of a Christian community is erroneous. However, look at almost any church newsletter and you will discover that congregations still think in these terms. The primary focus of the congregations seems to be upon 11:00 o'clock, Sunday mornings. Some newsletters even report the Sunday attendance, encourage the delinquent to attend next Sunday morning, and report the offerings for last Sunday. Of course, this is followed by the admonition that offerings "are not what they should be." Implied in all of this is the notion that the primary life of the congregation is contained in a one-hour period, one day a week, during corporate worship.

What we are contending is that that hour on Sunday is the time when the congregation expresses its corporate life; that is very different from what is described above. Martin Marty, church historian, has said that "a worship service for a visitor ought to be like seeing the huddle at a football game. You know something is going on, but all you can see is their rear ends." The huddle, of course, should not be so tight that you know you cannot get into it. Rather, the invitation should be to join the huddle. In that coming together, an involved and important milieu of relationships is being expressed. If you are not included in that web of relationships, you will feel like an outsider. The Christian parish community expressing itself this way need not apologize for the fact that the casual worshiper feels like an outsider. That is only natural, if worship is expressing truly a common life of a common people.

Another false assumption about worship is that it ought to function as a factory turning out mass-produced Christians. Worship, it seems to me, is not the setting in which a common life and faith are produced; rather it is the occasion to express that life and faith which is already a part of the community. When the church wants to teach, the classroom, the study session, and the small group discussion seem appropriate places for that. In worship we should be doing something different: expressing faith and celebrating it.

Some faithful churchgoers view worship as a spiritual filling station. They see worship as a gulp of fresh air which will keep them safe for a week in the smog of a God-less world. With regard to the notion that God is present only in the sanctuary, let me say quite bluntly: that is heresy. It is not the only place where he is to be found. Instead, we should come to celebrate with other people the fact that we have been with him all week in the world. William Stringfellow speaks eloquently to this notion in the following statement:

> He [the Christian] participates not because public worship is a good thing in itself or because he "gets something out of it," but rather to celebrate, to enjoy, to dramatize, and to announce the presence and action of God in the world—not in the sanctuary. The sanctuary is almost the last place God visits, and he certainly isn't confined to sanctuaries built by men.

> The enlivened layman is not religious, but he honors the Incarnation—the news that God has entered, is active in, and is concerned for both immediately and ultimately the common life of this world. The place therefore, where the Christian encounters God is out there—on the street, in the real world, as it really is.[2] [Brackets by J.E.S.]

This is a word that all congregations of worshiping Christians must hear!

Joe Mathews of the Ecumenical Institute in Chicago has a positive perspective on worship. He made the following prediction about the place of worship in his projection of the church, twenty years hence:

> Worship, of course, [will be there]. In our day, something tremendous has happened in that the secular world has discovered the importance of symbols. No man can be an authentic person until, in a disciplined fashion, he can dramatize his self-understanding. So worship is the key. Proclamation, the verbalization of the good news that all is good, that you are totally accepted, that everything is approved, that the future

is possible and open—that has to be done. I *already know* that I am accepted, but I *do not really know* it until I hear you, my brothers, say it.[3] [Brackets by J.E.S.]

Proclamation has to be a part of worship. That is why the passing of the peace as an act of worship is so important. The handclasp of shalom (peace) that goes with it is the affirmation of my acceptance. I need to receive that from the community. I know I am forgiven, but I don't really know it until my brothers and sisters tell me so again and again.

Corporate celebration, of course, will be expressed in many forms as communities respond to God's grace in and through their common life. We have said something about the nature of worship and of the manner in which the parish community can approach and participate in it. Let us now mention the role of the pastor in this corporate celebration. My contention is that his or her role should be primarily that of *prompter.*

An obvious and immediate question arises: can the pastor be prompter when he or she stands in a pulpit three feet above criticism? Can the pastor be a prompter when the pulpit overshadows the font; when the altar or communion table is difficult to locate? Can the pastor function as a prompter when the Reformation has left him or her with only an academic robe? Can the pastor be a prompter when the people sit in pews without facing one another? Can the pastor be a prompter when all the congregation can see is the pastor? These are difficult, but very important, questions.

To speak of the pastor as prompter automatically calls into question church architecture, vestments, and a host of other traditions. I am willing to call these into question. Questioning does not imply or suggest that these traditions must be eliminated; it merely says that questions about them must be raised.

If people are going to celebrate corporately and express their common lives, then the clergyman or clergywoman, as officiant and celebrator, has to allow the laity to carry the action. This can be done in several ways. In fact, it has become the source of renewal in some parishes. For example, women bake bread for the sacrament. Others make wine. Banners which hang in the sanctuary are made by people in the congregation, and the laity even have begun to write some of the hymns. Young people in blue jeans play guitars and dance as part of the celebration.

In the area of liturgical renewal, some efforts appear to be gimmicks. Sometimes the guitar hymns are maudlin, and the theology contained therein is wretched. In other words, worship is not renewed simply by introducing guitars and banners. But on the other hand, much that is being done in liturgical reforms is exciting and genuinely expressive. Many congregations have become involved in developing liturgies which express truly the corporate life of the community.

An example would perhaps demonstrate more clearly what I have in mind. I am thinking of a parish in which the liturgy is extremely "high church" for a Protestant congregation, but where the liturgical prayers are really the prayers of the church—the people. Every Saturday ten laymen (different ones each week) gather for a few hours to write liturgical petitions so that when the congregation comes to the altar for prayer on Sunday morning, the prayers of the church are the corporate prayers of at least ten members of that parish community. In this particular parish, in that very "straight" setting, there has been a genuine effort to involve the people in the worship. We can all learn from this. Until worship becomes more fully this kind of corporate expression, congregations will never become Christian communities.

For the pastor to preside as prompter can be a very difficult task; one for which liturgical training does not prepare the clergyman or clergywoman. The challenge of renewal, it seems to me, is for pastor and parish to break new ground together in the matter of liturgical forms of celebration. Corporate celebration is one of the marks of a healthy Christian community. It is an event in which both pastor and laity must be involved if corporateness is to mean something in fact.

A Corporate Action

The third characteristic of a healthy Christian community is participation in corporate action outside the community; in other words, mission. For most parishes, this is the most difficult aspect of community to incorporate into a corporate life. Too many congregations assume that it is optional, rather than essential. The issue of involvement in the world lies at the heart of the Christian faith and of church renewal.

Rev. Gordon Cosby of the Church of the Savior in Washington, D. C. illustrates the relationship between renewal and involvement by comparing it to a dance step. In some dances, steps are described in terms of a moving foot and a standing foot. "Church renewal comes when you understand that the 'given,' the standing foot, for the church is not in its structures, with involvement being the moving foot as an option. Renewal takes place when that shifts. When you realize the 'given' is involvement in the real life of the world, you can play with the structures that help you implement that." Renewal takes that kind of shift in attitude.

Earlier, William Stringfellow, the lay theologian, was quoted regarding the nature of worship. Now he helps us explore the relationship between worship and involvement. Regarding this, Christians need to understand the priorities of each as they live out their Christianity in the world. Any Christian community intent upon living its collective life with new intentionality, needs to examine these words:

> We gather now and then in sanctuaries, not because God has been waiting for us, but in order to announce to each other and to the world our experience and enjoyment of the presence of God outside. There's no other reason for coming to church. Unlike religious men who need to come as they say, for the sake of their souls, or their justification, the Christian man comes to the sanctuary and truly participates in the worship of God only as he is involved empirically, actually, and radically in the common life of the world, in whatever form his particular involvement may take. Worship which is cut off from the real life of the world is not worship, but idolatry, no matter how true the words offered. Maybe, worship in the sanctuary, the religious form of the Christian life in its stylized sense, is authenticated only by a profound involvement in the life of the world, where God is, after all, himself involved.[4]

This essential nature of involvement as a mark of the Christian life needs to be emphasized because, for the Christian and the Christian community, self-preservation is the greatest potential heresy.

It always has been. Self-preservation goes on faster and dries harder than the latest house paint, so to speak. It creeps in the moment we make tough decisions.

The radical scandal of the cross is that it denies self-preservation. We will always look naive in the eyes of the world if we are faithful. We will always appear to be suckers. If I understand the New Testament, we will always be advocates of the pariah, the outcast. Christians will always find themselves among the lepers and the untouchables. These things will be in evidence if we are to be part of an authentic, faithful community of Christ.

But this makes life very difficult, especially the Christian life. The minute I know that my faithfulness requires these kinds of risks I also start worrying about my pension plan. The moment I start to be prophetic in the tradition of the Old Testament prophets, I hear the warning: "There is no prophet with a wife and four kids." These are just some of the tendencies toward self-preservation of which we need to be aware. I need to be reminded often that the essence of the Christian gospel is risk. If a Christian community is to be a renewed community, then its life must exist for the sake of the world's life. That is the scandal of the cross—a love which expands humanness beyond the limitations of the self.

Mr. David Gill, of the World Council of Churches, visited Washington, D.C. recently as part of a commission that was formulating a position paper on the proper role of the Christian church in the nineteen seventies. The commission had meetings with some of the world's leading theologians. There were over one hundred preliminary statements on the church's role which were initially advanced. After a year, there remained only two statements on which there was any consensus. The first was: "The church aligns itself with the poor and the oppressed." The second was: "Noninvolvement is a nonoption."

With these assumptions the church as Christian community must begin. Perhaps no more are needed. The church must always align itself with the poor and the oppressed. Noninvolvement is a nonoption. Often the church, in fear of making a wrong commitment, remains uncommitted. In this there are two errors. First, there is no position like noncommitment; there is only the question as to what one is committed to. And secondly, Christians must begin to believe that wrong commitments, when they happen, will be forgiven by the grace of God, which all Christians say they believe.

What ought to be the role of the pastor in this vital area of corporate action outside immediate parish life? It seems to me that he or she is called to be an *enabler.* This is what Saint Paul meant when he said in Ephesians, chapter four: "And his gifts were that some are pastors for the equipping of the saints for their ministry."

The pastor is one who equips people for their ministry and one who, then, participates with them in it. But as he or she participates, the background should be where that involvement takes place most often. As a pastor in the Community of Christ, this was very difficult for me to learn to do. Perhaps an illustration will communicate the point. A very capable woman kept saying for nearly a year and a half: "Be my Bishop; give me my assignment; put me on a committee." I had almost given in when she conceived of an idea called "Home Buyers." Since that time thirty-five families have moved into their own homes which they are now in the process of buying—because of one woman. She found her ministry instead of having me assign her one.

In the Community of Christ we also saw the beginning of a Montessori school. A young man had the idea; the community helped evoke his gift of teaching. In this both the pastor and the Christian community had a role; but it was someone else's dream. The pastor of a community is there to enable others to implement their dreams—to help them find their own unique area of service. And the congregation's task is to develop these areas of service for themselves and others.

As I began my ministry at the Community of Christ, I made the decision not to be the central person in any one of our ministries; not to assume the traditional role of pastor which I had been conditioned to accept and which others expected of me. In retrospect, none of the activities of the Community of Christ has centered upon me. All of the programs have originated in the dreams of some other members of the community. A healthy congregation is one wherein the pastor remembers that he or she is an enabler for ministry; it is one in which the members of the community understand themselves to be ministers, too.

A World with Hope and with God

This essay began with the reminder that Saint Paul shared with the church at Ephesus: that Christians are new members of the community of Israel, which is a covenant and covenanting people. The Christian community lives in the world with hope and with God. This suggests to me that a Christian theology of hope is based in the community of faith. A common faith which finds continual expression in celebration and in corporate action is a cogent description of what it means to be such a community of Christ. The parish or congregation which defines and structures its corporate life in these terms has discovered the vital core of church renewal. The pastor who understands his or her function as that of witness, prompter, and enabler is freed to allow and encourage the parish community to design a corporate life which expresses its faith in celebration and action. The true pastor enables the congregation to be ministers—to find support for their dreams. And the real congregation dreams together and acts in Christ's name in the world.

NOTES

1. Robert McAllister, "The Psychology of Community," in *Experiments in Community,* a collection of papers delivered at the Twenty-eighth North American Liturgical Week (Washington, D.C.: The Liturgical Conference, 1968), p. 78.

2. William Stringfellow, "The Authentic Christian," *Faith At Work,* 78, no. 2 (March 1965): p. 26. Reprinted by permission from *Faith at Work,* 1000 Century Plaza, Suite 210, Columbia, Maryland 21044.

3. Joseph W. Mathews, "Joseph Mathews on Church Renewal," *Together,* 10, No. 3 (March 1966), p. 50. Reprinted from *Together* Magazine, March 1966; copyright © 1966 by The Methodist Publishing House.

4. Stringfellow, "The Authentic Christian," pp. 26–27. Reprinted by permission.

The fundamental problem is that we are not at all the "Christian" nation we like to think we are, but essentially a secular one. The paradox is that most church people do not know this, and if someone tells them so, they do not believe it. We have practically identified the purposes of the church with the life and goals of the nation. This is evidence of captivity to culture—not obedience to Christ.

C. C. GOEN
"The Cultural Captivity
of the American Churches"

8 The Believers' Church and Catholicity in the World Today

Rosemary R. Ruether

Not too many years ago, writers on the church could still speak confidently of a certain spectrum of different types of ecclesiology ranging from right to left, from sacerdotal forms related to imperial concepts of Christendom, to reformed types related to the European nation state, to left wing Anabaptist and Spiritualist forms which rejected church–state relationships for a free church polity. This spectrum of ecclesiological views could reasonably be supposed to correspond to existing denominations. But both long term shifts in the relationship between church and state, religion and culture, in European society, plus more recent and dramatic reawakenings within traditional churches are rendering this typology obsolete.

CHRISTIANITY TODAY

First of all, the secularization of the state, in progress since the late eighteenth century, reflecting shifts in the relationship between religion and culture from at least a hundred years earlier, have gradually dissolved the construct of church and state known as Christendom. With the tie between citizenship and church membership loosened and disappearing, all churches of every tradition find themselves essentially in the situation of being "free" churches or voluntary societies.

Secondly, movements of renewal within historical Catholic and Protestant churches are producing communities of radical Christians within and across the boundaries of all these communions. Finally, the traditional believers' churches of the left wing of the Reformation and the Puritan Revolution find that they too, in their own way, have become historical churches, with traditions, with forms that become timeworn, with means of institutional self-perpetuation which do not depend solely on the personal faith and commitment of the believers, and so they too must speak of a renewal within an institutionally and historically conditioned membership. Thus, although there are certainly many reminders, in terms of various forms of ecclesiastical organization and ideology, which hark back to that spectrum of differing ecclesiologies represented by the spectrum of denominations, in terms of what is actually going on, this spectrum is becoming obsolete.

All existing churches, from Roman Catholic to Quaker, are finding themselves in the roughly comparable position of having certain institutional and ideological apparatus on their hands which may not speak to the rising generation, and, at the same time, having to face the radical question of what it means to be Christians in a world which does not know Christ, even if it has, at one time or another, learned to use his name on its coins and public buildings. This is a precious moment of opportunity for the renewal of the Christian spirit, but one which could easily be lost in false or secondary forms of renewal such as institutional, corporative mergers or the restitution of past cultural landmarks.

THE MESSIANIC VISION

The fundamental question of the existence of the church in the world is the question of the existence of the messianic community in history. The messianic community is essentially the revolutionary community which is born in an experience of radical rejection of the false, inauthentic principles of existence of the prevalent society, including its religious forms, and which reaches out to a reborn humanity. The dominant society lives under the law of sinful or inauthentic life, which has fallen out of communion with God and with each other, and which organizes itself under a "law and order" that is actually but systematized disorder. This systematized disorder is the systematization of man's alienation from God, from nature, from his fellowman and ultimately from himself.

Man's authentic being is founded upon the Spirit of God. God as Creator Spirit pours forth his being into the world to create a community of beings who exist only because they rest upon this gift of divine being. The mystery of created being lies in the fact that its nature is to be both contingent and yet free. Created being has no self-subsistent being of its own, but it exists only through that gift of being which it receives from God. Yet it is free to relate or not to relate itself to its divine source of being. Created being exists authentically only by freely accepting life as a gift, freely willing to live by grace or by faith alone, and thereby opening its being to its transcendent source and becoming a transparent vehicle or presence of God in the world. This openness of human being to God is expressed and experienced existentially in an openness to our fellowman and the created world around us. "He who says he loves God, and hates his brother is a liar, for how can you love God, whom you have not seen, if you do not love your brother, whom you have seen" (I John 4:20). We must also include a loving, nonexploitative relationship to nature in this picture as well, for this is a dimension that has often been lost in the Christian account of faith and sin, but it is very much a part of the biblical perspective.

Man's fall or sinfulness consists essentially in an inward turn of the self upon itself; a kind of self-grasping and self-enclosure which wills to live as if it were "like God"; that is, as if it were a transcendent, autonomous being which could be founded upon itself and stood in no need of grace. This was the temptation whispered in the ear of the mother of the human race by the serpent. But it is a false promise, because in seeking to grasp his own being as an autonomous possession, man moves off the authentic ground of his being and falls into a self-enclosure which, at its core, is emptiness or death. Man falls away from the authentic foundation of his being and encoils himself upon that emptiness or nothingness from whence he came when God created the world out of nothing. He is still externally held in existence by God, to be sure, but inwardly he has become hollow, and his inauthentic self-grasping is now expressed in exploitative, oppressive relationships with his fellowman. As he himself becomes an assertive ego, alienated from the true foundation of his being, so also his fellow men become objects of manipulation, rather than persons to be received in grace and thanksgiving.

This alienated, exploitative relationship also extends to his dealings with nature and with God as well, for God, too, becomes an object to be employed in power plays with others. All reality becomes fuel for exploitation. The rape of nature, the pollution of our mother the earth and our father the sky, the stinking streams where no fish can breathe, the smoking sky where no bird can fly, the trash-strewn streets of the blackened city where children's cries testify to the collective effect of man's fallen nature. Nature falls through the fall of man and all are in slavery together, groaning for release from this bondage to decay. As Saint Paul puts it:

> For the creation waits with eager longing for the revealing of the sons of God; for the creation was subjected to futility, not of its own will but by the will of him who subjected it in hope; because the creation itself will be set free from its bondage to decay and obtain the glorious liberty of the children of God. We know that the whole creation has been groaning in travail together until now; and not only the creation, but we ourselves, who have the first fruits of the Spirit, groan inwardly as we wait for adoption as sons, the redemption of our bodies. (Rom. 8:20–23)

The salvation of man, in both the biblical perspective and the Marxist revolutionary perspective, is also a restoration of man to communion with nature and nature to communion with itself. It is the "resurrection of nature."[1] It is the peaceable kingdom of the biblical perspective, which includes not only man's inward obedience to God's word, but brotherhood, the forging of swords into plowshares, the reconciliation of man and nature where the lion lies down with the lamb and the little child leads them, and where earth itself is transfigured in beauty and fecundity and ceases to live by the law of tooth and claw. These sensuous, pictorial images in the prophets, which have often embarrassed Christians in their "materialism," express that biblical insight that salvation is not simply a matter of the soul, but of the whole man, nature and society; the reconciliation and transfiguration of all created reality in a community with each other that raises up a cosmic dance and feast of praise to its heavenly Father.

The church, then, or the messianic community, is essentially the community born in an ever new resurgence of this vision of total salvation. Having grasped and indeed been reborn in its vision and hope for what man and creation ought to be, it reacts with prophetic wrath to that inauthenticity, those oppressive and exploitative forms which exist as the prevalent mode of life of the world. Its vision is a radical vision because it perceives that this inauthentic life is not a superficial aberration that is easily reformed by corrections in the existing system, but rather goes to the very foundations of the system itself. The very principles upon which the system is founded assume an alienated, exploitative relationship between man and man. Renewal then must be radical renewal which goes to the roots of the system and refounds it upon a new and radically different principle of existence, that of brotherhood and agapic love. This is why the messianic tradition is essentially a radical tradition, the root of the revolutionary tradition in Western society and societies influenced by the Judaeo-Christian messianic heritage.

Those in whom the messianic vision and hope have been reborn, then, find themselves pitted against the surrounding society in a fundamental way, and this includes that religious society which calls itself church, but which the radical soon perceives to live by a principle of existence which is not essentially different from that of the world and to be indeed little more than the religious ratification of the status quo. From the standpoint of the world, including the churches of the world, the Christian, then, is a madman, a dreamer, a clown, a criminal, a man maladjusted to reality as it is presently constituted. All the guardians of the status quo, the policemen, judges, generals, administrators, priests, psychologists, and teachers, tell him he is wrong, all wrong; that he must adjust himself to things as they are. But in defiance of every reality, the Christian lives by a different vision and his soul vibrates to a different tune. He lives by faith in a world unseen, in fidelity to things which do not yet exist.

It is in this spirit that the Chicago 15 (one of a series of Christian radical groups, mostly Roman Catholic, who broke into draft offices and other offices and destroyed property symbolic of the military machine) have entered a plea of "insanity" in the courts. They entered this plea not seriously, but in the spirit of high Christian jest, for they know that it is the world around them and not they who are insane. It was Agnew with his pompous and murderous polemics, Nixon with his incredible rationalizations and covert hopes, the military machine which serves up the count of small dead Asiatic bodies like a football score to the folks at home; it is these that are insane. It is a government which has given over sixty-seven percent of its national resources to a mounting calculation of terror, while progressively sacrificing the elemental well-being of its own people in the name of "national security," which is insane. It is a society which buys more and more locks and guns for its segregated suburbs and more and more mace and artillery for its police to contain the hunger, miseducation and wrath of the slums that its delinquent affluence has created, which is insane. Therefore to be sane is to cut through this intolerable charade and pretence and to grasp the obvious, and thereby to become a madman, a conspirator, a traitor and a criminal in the eyes of the systematized disorder of this world. In a world where all the good church people live by the law of madness, only the madman can be sane. This is why intrepid Christian lawbreakers, destroyers of the sort of property which calculates the number of bodies to be fed into the war machine each month, appear before a judge, and choking back simultaneous laughter and tears, solemnly plead "cultural insanity" as the cause of their misdeed.

The messianic vision can never be a form of private or individual salvation. By nature it seeks community; it seeks a brotherhood which shares and lives in this vision. It is a vision, not of the solitary flight of the alone to the alone, but of a new humanity on a new earth that will overcome the old forms of existence of this world. Those who share this vision must seek each other out, and found a visible society which attempts to make concrete and visible the beginning of this new world. The messianic kingdom cannot remain simply an idea, an ideal kingdom cultivated in inwardness by solitary saints. It must open up a real liberated zone in the world, and exhibit itself as a real possibility for human life made visibly present in a time, a place, a people. As Daniel Cohn-Bendit, the French leader of the student strike of 1968, said of the revived utopian socialist hopes of that revolutionary experience:

> What matters is not working out a reform of capitalist society, but launching an experiment that completely breaks with that society, an experiment that will not last, but which allows a glimpse of a possibility; something is revealed for a moment and then vanishes. But that is enough to prove that something could exist.[2]

CHURCH AS SEPARATED COMMUNITY

This vision of possibility is the essence of the believers' church as a gathered community. It is a gathered community, not because it consists of people with the same temperament, the same culture, the same ethnic background, or the same style and language in expressing the faith. It is a gathered community because all share the same spirit and the same commitment. That, above all differences in class, culture, race or creed, means they find a brotherhood in a common vision and a willingness to commit themselves to a new, radical life-style appropriate to this vision; a radical life-style which may also put them in many kinds of jeopardy with the powers and principalities of this world. They are the community of those who are willing to put their lives on the line to venture a new possibility for human existence, and to run the risks of ostracism and persecution that this may raise in their relation with the dominant structures of society which do not allow for such a possibility.

It is this level of commitment which is the essence of the believers' church as a disciplined, committed fellowship. But this fellowship is radically nonsectarian and ecumenical vis-à-vis the class, cultural, racial and religious groupings of the world. All the alienated ways in which men are separated into classes, tribes, churches, nations, clubs and cliques to stand against each other, excluding, oppressing and rejecting a common humanity with each other, these are all rejected and dissolved. Men learn to recognize their brothers across every barrier of religion, race, class and culture. Men drop their guns and reach across trenches built by mutual suspicion to grasp hands. Men drop the masks of superiority and denigration to encounter one another as persons. The wall of silence created by exploitation and subservience is broken and dialogue begins.

In this sense, the believers' church is radically catholic, radically ecumenical, universalist in its anthropology and outreach. It recognizes no extrinsic tests of membership, but only that intrinsic test which automatically gathers those who seek light and repels those who are not willing to have their own existences tested by its searing flame. It is, in this existential sense, often misunderstood as sectarianism, that the Gospel of John speaks of the children of light and the children of darkness, and warns that the world, which rejects the possibility of an agapic fellowship, will throw them out of its churches and even count it a service to God if it kills them (John 16:1–3).

The believers' church, then, is a separated people, not because of any inner sectarianism in its own life principle, but because it must exist in tension and conflict with a world formed along alien and hostile principles of existence, a world which instinctively recognizes the community of believers as a threat to the status quo, and to the foundations of its authority and power. The more clearly the believing community grasps its own principle of life, the more they will stand out against the system around them. The more they really live by those principles, the more they run the risk of being a dissident and even outlaw community vis-à-vis the "law and order"; that is to say, the systematized disorder of the system. Although the believers' church is itself radically catholic, nonsectarian and universalist, and recognizes no test of brotherhood except brotherhood itself, yet it is precisely this principle that causes it to become a dissident community vis-à-vis a world which lives by the law of enmity and exploitation. No greater dissent can be offered to a society than to refuse to accept its enemies as your own enemies. The believers' church must be both radical and catholic, and so can merge and identify with the world only when the world itself is transformed, loses every vestige of sinfulness, and merges into that new form of the world which is called the Kingdom of God. The believers' church is the avant-garde of a new world. It is the beginning of the new humanity which will become the form of the new creation when the fallen world of powers and principalities is finally overcome. It is for this reason that it is truly the church, the ecclesia, the messianic community, the first fruits of the resurrection from the death, sojourning within this present world, but as an earnest and prefigurement of the world to come.

THE OLD AGE AND THE NEW AGE

All this, then, we can say about the believers' church according to its essential nature. But having said all these good things, we have then to recognize the problematical nature of the existence of the messianic community in history. The messianic community leaps out ecstatically to a new possibility and a new world which has not yet come, and experiences in its own birth the overcoming of the world of powers and principalities, the coming of Christ, and the dawning of the new age. But the form of the old age still persists around it. The mysteries of time, history and finitude continue, and these are strangely mixed with externality, manipulative and rote modes of existence which do not merely rule the world around us, but continue to possess our own souls as well. Therefore the messianic community exists only in a provisional and proleptical sense. It cannot historically perpetuate itself, but can only be reborn from above in the freedom of the Spirit. Even at its best, it has only a tenuous foothold on the new world, and most of its life is still controlled by the old forms of existence. Even to keep the clarity of its own vision, it must live in constant repentance and the renewal of its mind. Therefore, even when rejected by that oppressive society around it which is offended by its new life-style, it recognizes its human solidarity with that same sinful humanity. It knows that whatever insight it possesses, it has as an undeserved gift and knows that behind the facade of the enemy there lies only the more deeply buried brother. So it must reject all self-righteousness, and reach out with a passion for humanity which is even more jealous for the unrevealed humanity of its oppressor than it is for its own humanity. To do less than this would be to subvert the basis of its own humanity and thereby the very principles on which the revolution rests. Without that final love which loves the enemy, breaking through the facade of enmity to the lost brother underneath, every revolution is betrayed and becomes merely a reversal of the reversal in which oppressor and oppressed change places, but nothing fundamentally is changed.

The believers' church must recognize not only its continued solidarity with sinful humanity as its own lost brotherhood, but also its continued subservience to the mysteries of time and finitude as well. A spark has been lit; a struggle commenced; a liberated zone opened up and momentarily subsisting, but men grow weary, the vision fades, the liberated zone congeals into a new tribe, sect, club or clique. Membership cards are passed out according to hair-style, dress, manners or adherence to the formulas written down by the elders. So the messianic community, if it is to be true to its nature, within the present form of the world, must accept the radically provisional and proleptic form of its own possibility of existence. It cannot perpetuate this principle of existence horizontally, but can only be reborn from above. It can fashion no institutional guarantees to perpetuate the Spirit through channels of tradition, ordination or succession, for the Spirit can never become the chairman of the board of trustees of anyone's institution. The Spirit is a free spirit; it blows where it will, and appears wherever it appears, not at the duly appointed times and places, when popes are sitting on the proper chairs, ex cathedra, and everyone is in his Sunday best, but it shows up at all sorts of improper times and unexpected places. The community of believers appears, not in the White House parlor where all is in order, but in a motley gathering in the streets beyond the barricades, where the paddy wagons are hurrying to arrest the illegal worshippers who kneel without permit in the park banned to public assembly. It does no good to plead that we are Abraham's sons and Christ's vicars, for the Spirit bypasses these hallowed pedigrees and raises up new children of God and heirs of Christ from the streets.

The believers' church cannot perpetuate its rebirth in the Spirit through historical succession, and yet it is not born without history or tradition, for, wherever it rises, it recognizes its solidarity with all the brotherhoods that have gone before it. These would include not only radical Christians from the first Pentecostal assembly, through perhaps a shattered line of apocalypticists, spiritualists, monks, mystics, and brotherhoods through the Middle Ages on into the pedigrees of the Left Wing of the Reformation and perhaps Christian radicals of the peace and freedom struggles today, but also other groups, alienated from religious language, who shared the same impulse, especially utopian and communalist socialists of the nineteenth century and today. We might think, then, of the radical heritage as "brotherhoods of the kingdom," brotherhoods of the vision of the new humanity. Yet the radical community must realize that, as these groups recovered a vision and commenced a struggle, so they also passed and became only historical memory, or perhaps became founders of organizations which used their name but departed far from their vision. And so it behooves us not to be too narrow in our cultural sympathies, for what is today's iconoclasm may be tomorrow's ratification of the status quo.

A radical church should be ecumenical in its cultural sympathies, open to all insights from every branch of the Christian heritage, as well as secular culture and other religions which can give us insight into the meaning of authentic humanity. But the radical church may also engage in its own cultural struggle and even fashion new instruments of organization, transmission and ministry which can furnish a handle and a criterion for the correct discernment of the heritage. The danger comes only when it does this in such a way as to narrow the cultural base for future generations, conceiving of the heritage only in terms of the history which its own group is now making. Those secondary structures of institutionalization and tradition have a place in our account of the church precisely because we remain in history. They must be valued for what they can do; namely, to pass down the ideas, the experiences, the true and false experiments of the past. They cannot transmit the Holy Spirit, but they can transmit a host of helpful clues and guides which we would do well to remember. We have to learn to be free to use the tradition, while rejecting its illicit claims to primary and perpetual authority, and we have to be free to launch new experiments while knowing that the experiment should last only so long as the spirit of those who gave it birth lasts. We have a right to try to fashion better, freer, simpler, more communal forms of transmission which will be more appropriate to the gospel than we may have inherited from the past, but we must also know that these too will become a tradition, which must be appropriated and used in unexpected ways by the next apostolic emissaries, and not just exactly as we would wish to decree, and so we too must not absolutize even our best insights. In the last analysis our faith and our freedom do not rest in these, but in the faithfulness of God who continually creates:

> In all these things we are more than conquerers through him who loved us. For I am sure that neither death, nor life, nor angels, nor principalities, nor things present, nor things to come, nor powers, nor height, nor depth, nor anything else in all creation will be able to separate us from the love of God in Christ Jesus Our Lord. (Rom. 8:37–39.)

NOTES

1. Erich Fromm, *Marx's Concept of Man; with a translation from Marx's Economic and Philosophical Manuscript by T. B. Bottomore with an Afterword by Erich Fromm* (New York: F. Ungar, 1966), p. 12.

2. Hervé Bourges, *The French Student Revolt: the Leaders Speak: Daniel Cohn-Bendit, Jean-Pierre Duteuil, Alain Geismar, Jacques Sauvageot,* trans. B. R. Brewster (New York: Hill and Wang, 1968), p. 81.

Contributors

Contributors

JEFFREY K. HADDEN: Professor in the Department of Anthropology and Sociology of the University of Virginia, Charlottesville, Virginia; author of numerous scholarly and popular articles; book review editor of "The Journal for the Scientific Study of Religion"; author of the important, recent study on conflicts among clergy and laity, *The Gathering Storm in the Churches;* one of the leading experts in the field of sociology of religion.

EDGAR W. MILLS: Director of the Ministry Studies Board, Department of Ministry of the National Council of Churches; an ordained minister in the United Presbyterian Church; coauthor of *Stress in Ministry* and *Ex-Pastors: Why Men Leave the Parish;* consultant on professions and professionalism, with particular expertise in the area of ministerial professions.

GARRY W. HESSER: Professor of Sociology, The College of Wooster, Wooster, Ohio; ordained minister of the Disciples of Christ and a former pastor; contributor to the "Journal for the Scientific Study of Religion" and "Pulpit Digest." His continuing research is in the area of professionalism among the clergy.

SIDNEY D. SKIRVIN: Dean of Students and Director of Academic Placement at Union Theological Seminary in New York; an ordained United Presbyterian clergyman and former pastor of a rural Colorado church and an urban church in Wilmington, Delaware. Dean Skirvin has done extensive scholarly and practical work in vocational counseling for clergy and seminary students. As a research interviewer he contributed to the recently-published study, *Ex-Pastors: Why Men Leave the Parish.*

C. C. GOEN: Professor of Church History at Wesley Theological Seminary in Washington, D. C.; author of a number of scholarly articles. His major work on *Revivalism and Separatism in New England, 1740-1800* was awarded the Brewer Prize of the American Society of Church History, 1962.

WILLIAM M. COSGROVE: Auxiliary Bishop of the Roman Catholic Diocese of Cleveland and a pastor at St. Henry's Parish; former Spiritual Director of Borromeo High School and College; and liaison with parishes for the "Social Justice Committee" of the Diocese of Cleveland.

A. JAMES ARMSTRONG: Bishop of the Dakotas Area of the United Methodist Church; former pastor at the Broadway Methodist Church in Indianapolis; author of *The Urgent Now, The Journey that Men Make,* and *Mission: Middle America*; former Chairman of the Peace Task Force of the United Methodist Council of Bishops.

JOHN E. SCHRAMM: Executive Director of Lutheran Social Services in Washington, D. C.; former pastor of the Community of Christ, an experimental ecumenical parish started by the American Lutheran Church; coauthor with David Anderson of *Dance in Steps of Change,* an account of parish life in the Community of Christ.

ROSEMARY R. RUETHER: Lay Roman Catholic theologian; professor of Historical Theology, Howard University School of Religion, Washington, D. C.; visiting lecturer, Yale Divinity School and Inter-Met, an experimental seminary in the nation's capital; author of numerous articles in popular and scholarly journals, and author of several books including *The Radical Kingdom, The Church Against Itself,* and *Liberation Theology.*